DEBATE Pro

Book 8

Author Jonathan S. McClelland
- BA in English with a Writing Concentration, University of South Carolina, Columbia, SC, USA
- Former English instructor at Daewon Foreign Language High School
- Current debate instructor for elementary school students
- Former curriculum developer at Korean Army Intelligence School
- Expert test developer of TOEFL, TOEIC, and TEPS

DEBATE Pro Book 8

Publisher Chung Kyudo
Editors Hong Inpyo, Cho Sangik
Proofreader Michael A. Putlack
Designers Zo Hwayoun, Park Sunyoung, Park Narae

First Published in February 2015
By Darakwon, Inc.
Darakwon Bldg., 211, Munbal-ro, Paju-si, Gyeonggi-do 10881
Republic of Korea
Tel: 82-2-736-2031 (Ext. 250)
Fax: 82-2-732-2037

Copyright © 2015 Darakwon, Inc.

All rights reserved. No part of this publication may be reproduced, stored in a retrieval system, or transmitted in any form or by any means, electronic, mechanical, photocopying, or otherwise, without the prior consent of the copyright owner. Refund after purchase is possible only according to the company regulations. Contact the above telephone number for any inquiry. Consumer damages caused by loss, damage etc. can be compensated according to consumer dispute resolution standards announced by the Korea Fair Trade Commission. An incorrectly collated book will be exchanged.

ISBN 978-89-277-0747-9 58740
978-89-277-0677-9 58740 (set)

www.darakwon.co.kr

Components Main Book / Workbook
10 9 8 7 6 5 4   23 24 25 26 27

Instilling Knowledge and Skills
for Thoughtful Debate

DEBATE Pro

Book 8

DARAKWON

Preface

The *Debate Pro* series is designed to provide students with an intermediate EFL ability with a sound understanding of a variety of debate topics and develop their speaking, listening, and critical thinking skills through debate. The series consists of eight sets of books, each of which includes a Main Book and a Workbook. Each Main Book includes five chapters covering five debate skills. Within each chapter, there are two units which each cover different topics for a total of ten debate topics per book. The Workbook supplements the Main Book by helping students understand the topic more deeply, developing skills for making examples and doing research, and evaluating the debates. The Workbook can be used in class and for homework assignments.

In the book, every debate topic is introduced with a large color photograph relating to the topic. Students are asked to analyze the picture and formulate opinions about the topic through a series of six warm-up questions. The topic is then explained in more detail through a reading passage of about 300 words which briefly presents background information about the topic before outlining arguments in favor of and against the topic. The passages are followed by vocabulary and comprehension exercises. Students are then required to apply what they have learned from the passage to answer a series of in-depth questions relating to the debate topic. Following these questions, students are given opinion examples before learning the debate skill for each topic. Finally, students will have the chance to apply their knowledge to create a full debate with the assistance of sample arguments and a debate flow chart.

Each book provides free MP3 files with recordings of the reading passages and opinion examples for every unit. There is also a Teacher's Guide available at www.darakwon.co.kr that includes answer keys and sample answers for every unit as well as teaching tips and suggestions for supplementing the material.

The *Debate Pro* series has the following features:

- Ten different debate topics per book covering a range of themes including education, technology, relationships, and responsibility
- Reading passages which provide a general understanding of arguments both for and against the given topic
- Questions that require students to formulate arguments and supporting opinions about each topic
- Five different debate skills per book designed to improve students' critical thinking and speaking skills
- Sample opinions and argument examples which help students develop their own arguments
- Free MP3 files with recordings of all passages and sample opinions

Contents

About This Book _7

Chapter 1
Creating Expert Opinion Examples

- **Unit 01** Road Space Rationing in Downtown Areas _12
- **Unit 02** Outlawing Homeschooling _22

Chapter 2
Creating Statistical Examples

- **Unit 03** Cutting CEO Salaries _34
- **Unit 04** Free Internet Service for the Poor _44

Chapter 3
Creating Academic Studies Examples

- **Unit 05** Extending the School Year _56
- **Unit 06** Detaining the Mentally Ill _66

Chapter 4
Creating Effective Rebuttals

- **Unit 07** Free Trade Agreements _78
- **Unit 08** Colonizing Other Planets _88

Chapter 5
Creating Closing Speeches

- **Unit 09** Merit-Based Pay for Teachers _100
- **Unit 10** America as the World's Police _110

About This Book

Overview

Debate Pro main book consists of five chapters. Each chapter contains two units with each focusing on the same debate skill. Every unit is further subdivided into part A and part B. Part A, Learning about the Topic, introduces students to the topic of the unit and consists of approximately one hour of learning material. Part B, Debating the Topic, requires students to formulate their arguments and debate the topic of the unit. The total time required for Part B is also approximately one hour.

Introduction for each section

Warm-up

This part includes a picture related to the topic for students to analyze. The pictures are followed by six warm-up questions. The questions in Part A require students to analyze the picture and can be answered as a class. In Part B, students draw upon their knowledge about the topic to answer questions with a partner.

Reading Passage

This part consists of a single reading passage approximately 300 words in length. The passage introduces general background information about the topic and presents specific arguments with examples both in favor of and against the topic.

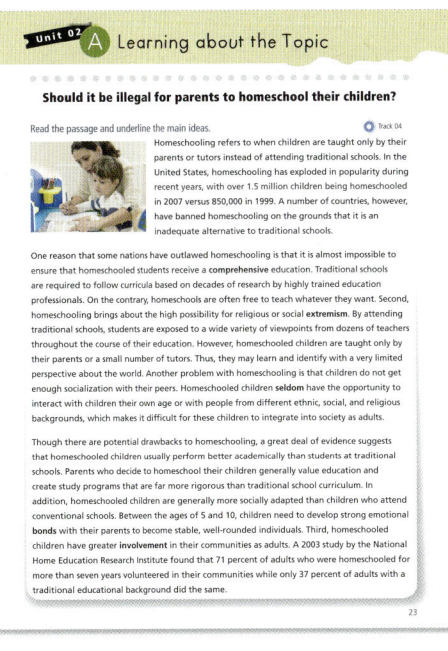

Vocabulary Check

Each reading passage is followed by five vocabulary questions to bolster students' vocabulary and ensure their understanding of the passage.

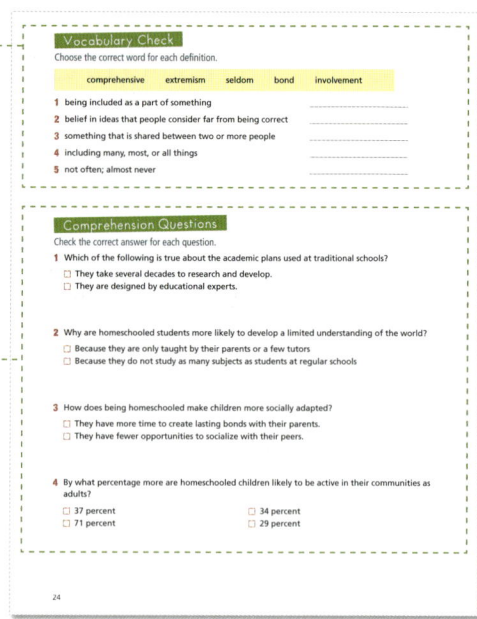

Comprehension Questions

Each reading passage includes four paired-choice reading comprehension questions. The questions ask students about the main idea of passage, factual information, and reasoning from the passage.

Questions for Debate

This portion consists of five open-ended questions related to the topic. The students must formulate opinions about each question and give reasons for their opinions. Key phrases are provided to help students improve their speaking skills.

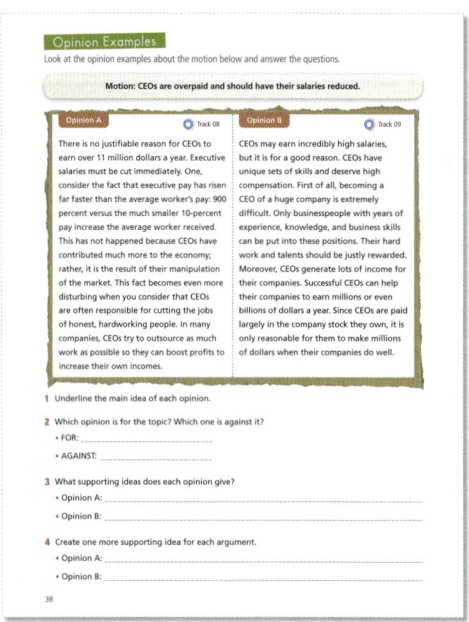

Opinion Examples

In this section, two opinion examples for and against the topic are provided. Students are required to understand the main idea of each example opinion and its supporting arguments. They must also provide an additional argument for each opinion.

Skills for Debate

This section introduces a debate skill and explains key concepts related to the topic. Each chapter focuses on a single debate skill across two units.

Practicing Debate Skills

This exercise follows each debate skill explanation to ensure that students understand the skill and can use it during their debate.

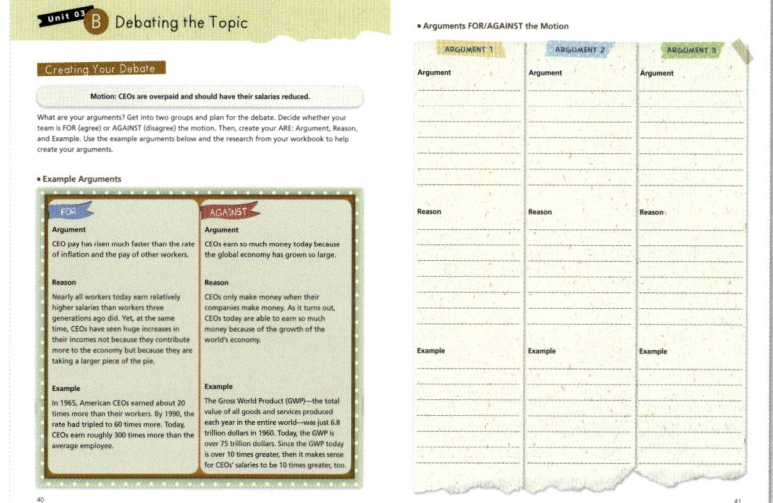

Creating Your Debate

This section begins by introducing the skills of ARE: Argument, Reason, and Example. Following this are two sample arguments, one for PRO and one for CON, with sample notes for the ARE. On the next page are three blank columns for students to work in teams and create their AREs.

Actual Debate

This portion consists of a debate flow chart. The chart outlines the order of debate and provides sample phrases to help students use proper debate language.

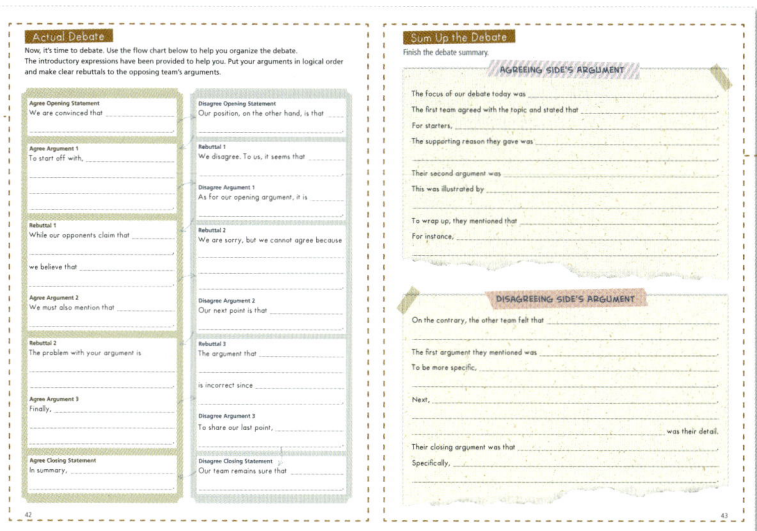

Sum Up the Debate

The final section requires students to summarize the arguments presented by both the PRO and CON teams during the debate. Sample phrases are given to help students.

Chapter 1

Creating Expert Opinion Examples

Unit 01 Road Space Rationing in Downtown Areas

Unit 02 Outlawing Homeschooling

Unit 01
Road Space Rationing in Downtown Areas

A. Discuss the following questions as a class.
1. What do you see in the picture above?
2. How would having so many cars on the road make commuting difficult?
3. What could be done to reduce the number of cars on this road?

B. Answer the following questions with a partner.
1. Does your city have a problem with too much traffic? Explain.
2. How does having so many cars in a small area negatively affect the environment?
3. Why is driving in downtown areas usually unnecessary?

Unit 01 A Learning about the Topic

Should cities ration road space in their downtown areas?

Read the passage and underline the main ideas.    Track 01

"In a successful modern city, the car must no longer be king." This is a quote by urban planner Patricia Brown. She believes that cities should implement road space rationing to reduce the number of cars in their downtown areas. This is generally achieved by allowing people to drive only on certain days of the week. Such restrictions would be simple to put into place and offer several attractive benefits for cities.

Perhaps the number one advantage of road space rationing would be the decrease in traffic **congestion**. The traffic in cities without driving restrictions is often highly congested, and this leads to excessively long commuting times. Road space rationing would significantly reduce the number of cars on the road and make driving times much shorter. Another clear advantage would be a reduction in pollution. In many downtown areas, the primary source of air pollution is automobiles. The carbon dioxide emitted by vehicles becomes trapped due to the large number of tall buildings. With fewer cars on the road, air quality will improve **drastically**. This has been the case in Mexico City and Sao Paulo. A final point to consider is that road space rationing would make downtown areas safer and more **pedestrian** friendly. For instance, in New York City's Times Square, the number of accidents where vehicles hit pedestrians was reduced by half after the city created a road rationing policy in the area.

For many cities, though, such driving restrictions are impractical. While the largest cities may have **extensive** public transportation systems that provide alternatives to driving, a number of smaller cities do not. As a result, people's commuting times would become longer since they would have to spend lots of time waiting for buses and trains to arrive. This leads to the next point: Citizens should have the right to drive cars if they want to. The right to own and drive a car is a fundamental personal liberty, and it is wrong for the government to dictate when people may use their cars. Lastly, road space rationing is simply not necessary. It is possible to make driving in downtown areas safer for cars and pedestrians by making tunnels for cars and **elevated** walkways for pedestrians. This allows traffic to flow more quickly while making it safer for pedestrians to walk in these areas.

Vocabulary Check

Choose the correct word for each definition.

> congestion   drastically   pedestrian   extensive   elevated

1 a person who is walking along a road
2 the state of being too full with something
3 very full or complete
4 raised above the ground
5 extreme in effect or action

Comprehension Questions

Check the correct answer for each question.

1 What is road space rationing according to the passage?
   ☐ Charging tolls for driving in downtown areas
   ☐ Limiting the days on which people may drive

2 Why is air pollution more likely to be a problem in downtown areas?
   ☐ Because these areas generally do not have many trees
   ☐ Because the air cannot escape due to the high-rise buildings

3 How did a driving restriction affect Times Square?
   ☐ Accidents between cars and people became 50 percent lower.
   ☐ The number of automobiles in the area was reduced by half.

4 In which case might people's commuting times increase?
   ☐ When a city does not have an extensive network of buses and subway trains
   ☐ When people still choose to drive their cars even when they are not supposed to

Questions for Debate

Think of and share ideas to explore the debatable issues in the article. Be sure to state your opinion clearly and to provide one supporting idea for each opinion.

1. Does your city have road space rationing? If so, do you think it is beneficial? If not, do you think it should be implemented?

   My city _____
   _____.

   My feeling about this is _____
   _____.

2. Why do you think traffic is such a major problem in downtown areas?

   To me, it seems that _____
   _____.

   In detail, _____
   _____.

3. How would people commute if they could not use their cars due to driving restrictions?

   It is possible for people to _____
   _____.

   This would be better because _____
   _____.

4. Why might road space rationing be considered a violation of people's personal liberty?

   Some people might feel that _____
   _____.

   More specifically, _____
   _____.

5. Aside from driving restrictions, how can cities reduce the number of cars in their downtown areas?

   Some of the alternatives include _____
   _____.

   These can be more effective because _____
   _____.

Opinion Examples

Look at the opinion examples about the motion below and answer the questions.

Motion: Cities should use road space rationing to reduce traffic in downtown areas.

Opinion A Track 02

I live in Beijing, which has a downtown road space rationing policy. Originally, the driving restriction was supposed to be only during the Olympics, but the city fortunately decided to continue the policy. The most obvious benefit is the improved air quality. Every day, about 20 percent of Beijing's vehicles are not allowed on the road. I read that this reduces vehicle emissions by more than 25 percent. Now, I don't need to wear my breathing mask every time I go outside. In addition, the driving restrictions have made the roads safer. There used to be over 200 accidents a day in the city. Now, there are fewer than 100 each day because of the road rationing policy.

Opinion B Track 03

While there are some reasonable arguments in favor of road rationing policies, I still oppose them. One reason is that they would be too difficult to enforce. The only way for cities to make sure that people aren't driving when they aren't supposed to is either by using surveillance cameras or by having police write lots of tickets. Both of these options are expensive and require a great deal of resources. Then there is the inconvenience of rationing policies for drivers. Sure, it may be possible to get around without a car in places like New York or London, but that cannot be done in cities without good public transportation like Los Angeles or Houston.

1 Underline the main idea of each opinion.

2 Which opinion is for the topic? Which one is against it?
- FOR: _____
- AGAINST: _____

3 What supporting ideas does each opinion give?
- Opinion A: _____
- Opinion B: _____

4 Create one more supporting idea for each argument.
- Opinion A: _____
- Opinion B: _____

Skills for Debate

Read and learn how to create expert opinion examples.

How Can You Create Expert Opinion Examples?

An **expert opinion** example is based on the ideas of researchers, scholars, professionals, and other experts in a given field. The purpose of using expert opinion examples is to support your argument with a fact or notion that has been proven true in the real world. As with all examples, it is important to focus on the most **relevant points** of the example to make it more convincing. You should also make sure to mention the **name of the expert** and **list that person's job title** to give your example more credibility.

Practicing Debate Skills

Read the following argument and expert opinion. Underline the parts of the passage that are relevant to the argument, and then use these ideas to create an expert opinion example.

- **Argument:** Restricting cars from downtown areas makes them more pedestrian friendly.

> **Expert Opinion – Andrew Minton, City Planner**
>
> Most downtown areas in the United States consist of large multilane streets with at-grade pedestrian crossings. While this design is often the most cost efficient, it is far from being the safest layout. To remedy this, I suggest that cities make two main changes to the design of their downtown areas. First, cities should create underpasses for their largest roads. These are essentially tunnels that allow busy roads to bypass smaller roads. This would greatly decrease the chances of pedestrians encountering cars on these roads. It has the added benefit of allowing traffic to flow much more efficiently. A second solution would be the creation of overpasses for pedestrians. The use of these bridges to bypass busy intersections would reduce vehicular-pedestrian accidents to nearly zero. To encourage pedestrians to use these overpasses, cities would have to build elevators and escalators for them. Building them would be a major investment, but since they would save many lives, they would be an investment worth making.

- **Example:** To make our point clearer, we will introduce the opinion of _____

Unit 01 B Debating the Topic

Creating Your Debate

Motion: Cities should use road space rationing to reduce traffic in downtown areas.

What are your arguments? Get into two groups and plan for the debate. Decide whether your team is FOR (agree) or AGAINST (disagree) the motion. Then, create your ARE: Argument, Reason, and Example. Use the example arguments below and the research from your workbook to help create your arguments.

■ Example Arguments

FOR

Argument

Restricting cars in downtown areas would reduce air pollution.

Reason

Automobiles emit carbon dioxide, a toxic chemical. Car emissions are an even bigger problem in downtown areas because of the high concentration of cars and tall buildings in these areas. Reducing the number of cars on the roads in downtown areas will decrease carbon dioxide emissions and make the air cleaner to breathe.

Example

Since the 2008 Olympics, Beijing has placed road rationing policies in its downtown area. In one study, restricting one-third of cars each day has reduced emissions by 40 percent.

AGAINST

Argument

Road space rationing is a violation of personal rights.

Reason

In a free society, people should have the right to drive their cars whenever they want. Road space rationing policies unfairly deny citizens of their right to drive. This is a clear violation of personal liberty and should not be tolerated.

Example

In countries where citizens have high levels of personal freedom, such as the United States and most nations in Western Europe, driving restriction laws go against the concept of being able to live how you want so long as you do not harm anyone else directly.

Arguments FOR/AGAINST the Motion

ARGUMENT 1

Argument

Reason

Example

ARGUMENT 2

Argument

Reason

Example

ARGUMENT 3

Argument

Reason

Example

Actual Debate

Now, it's time to debate. Use the flow chart below to help you organize the debate.
The introductory expressions have been provided to help you. Put your arguments in logical order and make clear rebuttals to the opposing team's arguments.

Agree Opening Statement
We are convinced that _____ .

Agree Argument 1
To start with, we feel that _____ .

Rebuttal 1
Your argument that _____ does not make sense because _____ .

Agree Argument 2
Second, it is our feeling that _____ .

Rebuttal 2
While you claim that _____, the fact is that _____ .

Agree Argument 3
Our last point is _____ .

Agree Closing Statement
As you can see, there is no doubt that _____ .

Disagree Opening Statement
On the contrary, our team believes that _____ .

Rebuttal 1
The problem with your idea is _____ .

Disagree Argument 1
First, we posit that _____ .

Rebuttal 2
Unfortunately, you are still wrong. Consider that _____ .

Disagree Argument 2
Our next argument is _____ .

Rebuttal 3
We strongly oppose the idea that _____ .

Disagree Argument 3
We will wrap up by mentioning that _____ .

Disagree Closing Statement
Our overall opinion remains that _____ .

Sum Up the Debate

Finish the debate summary.

AGREEING SIDE'S ARGUMENT

Our debate today dealt with _____.

The first team held the belief that _____.

First, they claimed that _____.

Their example was _____

_____.

The second argument they made was _____.

This was supported by _____

_____.

To conclude, they pointed out that _____.

Specifically, they stated that _____

_____.

DISAGREEING SIDE'S ARGUMENT

On the other hand, the second team believed that _____

_____.

They opened by mentioning that _____.

For instance, _____

_____.

Next, they pointed out that _____.

Their evidence was _____

_____.

Their final assertion was that _____.

_____

_____ was the proof they offered.

Unit 02 Outlawing Homeschooling

WARM-UP

A. Discuss the following questions as a class.

1. What do you see in the picture above?
2. Where do you think the girl is studying? Why do you think so?
3. How would learning at home be different from going to a regular school?

B. Answer the following questions with a partner.

1. Would you rather attend a traditional school or be homeschooled? Explain your choice.
2. How could students learn more when they are taught at home by their parents or tutors?
3. What are some ways that children could suffer by being homeschooled?

Unit 02 A Learning about the Topic

Should it be illegal for parents to homeschool their children?

Read the passage and underline the main ideas.  Track 04

Homeschooling refers to when children are taught only by their parents or tutors instead of attending traditional schools. In the United States, homeschooling has exploded in popularity during recent years, with over 1.5 million children being homeschooled in 2007 versus 850,000 in 1999. A number of countries, however, have banned homeschooling on the grounds that it is an inadequate alternative to traditional schools.

One reason that some nations have outlawed homeschooling is that it is almost impossible to ensure that homeschooled students receive a **comprehensive** education. Traditional schools are required to follow curricula based on decades of research by highly trained education professionals. On the contrary, homeschools are often free to teach whatever they want. Second, homeschooling brings about the high possibility for religious or social **extremism**. By attending traditional schools, students are exposed to a wide variety of viewpoints from dozens of teachers throughout the course of their education. However, homeschooled children are taught only by their parents or a small number of tutors. Thus, they may learn and identify with a very limited perspective about the world. Another problem with homeschooling is that children do not get enough socialization with their peers. Homeschooled children **seldom** have the opportunity to interact with children their own age or with people from different ethnic, social, and religious backgrounds, which makes it difficult for these children to integrate into society as adults.

Though there are potential drawbacks to homeschooling, a great deal of evidence suggests that homeschooled children usually perform better academically than students at traditional schools. Parents who decide to homeschool their children generally value education and create study programs that are far more rigorous than traditional school curriculum. In addition, homeschooled children are generally more socially adapted than children who attend conventional schools. Between the ages of 5 and 10, children need to develop strong emotional **bonds** with their parents to become stable, well-rounded individuals. Third, homeschooled children have greater **involvement** in their communities as adults. A 2003 study by the National Home Education Research Institute found that 71 percent of adults who were homeschooled for more than seven years volunteered in their communities while only 37 percent of adults with a traditional educational background did the same.

Vocabulary Check

Choose the correct word for each definition.

> comprehensive   extremism   seldom   bond   involvement

1. being included as a part of something _____
2. belief in ideas that people consider far from being correct _____
3. something that is shared between two or more people _____
4. including many, most, or all things _____
5. not often; almost never _____

Comprehension Questions

Check the correct answer for each question.

1. Which of the following is true about the academic plans used at traditional schools?
   - ☐ They take several decades to research and develop.
   - ☐ They are designed by educational experts.

2. Why are homeschooled students more likely to develop a limited understanding of the world?
   - ☐ Because they are only taught by their parents or a few tutors
   - ☐ Because they do not study as many subjects as students at regular schools

3. How does being homeschooled make children more socially adapted?
   - ☐ They have more time to create lasting bonds with their parents.
   - ☐ They have fewer opportunities to socialize with their peers.

4. By what percentage more are homeschooled children likely to be active in their communities as adults?
   - ☐ 37 percent
   - ☐ 71 percent
   - ☐ 34 percent
   - ☐ 29 percent

Questions for Debate

Think of and share ideas to explore the debatable issues in the article. Be sure to state your opinion clearly and to provide one supporting idea for each opinion.

1 Would you want to be homeschooled? Why or why not?

I would rather be _____

_____.

To go into more detail, _____

_____.

2 What subjects would like to learn about that you do not study at school?

The subjects that I would like to study are _____

_____.

To explain further, _____

_____.

3 Do you think children can become properly socialized when they do not attend school?

I am wholly convinced that _____

_____.

The reason I feel this way is _____

_____.

4 Homeschooled children have higher test scores on average. Why do you think this is?

Their test scores are probably better because _____

_____.

What I mean by this is _____

_____.

5 How can homeschooling children be more difficult for parents than sending their children to traditional schools?

It can be more difficult for parents since _____

_____.

This is a problem because _____

_____.

Opinion Examples

Look at the opinion examples about the motion below and answer the questions.

Motion: Homeschooling should be illegal.

Opinion A Track 05

I have never attended a traditional school, and I never want to. To me, being homeschooled is the only way to go. One of the best things about homeschooling is that it allows me to study the subjects I want at my own pace. In my case, I really enjoy biology, so my mom spends several hours each day teaching me about the subject, doing experiments with me, and so forth. Homeschooling is also more comfortable for me. I don't ever have to worry about being made fun of or dealing with peer pressure. The only people in my classes are my sister and me. This lets me focus on my studies and not get stressed about social problems.

Opinion B Track 06

As a teacher, I firmly oppose homeschooling. The biggest shortcoming of it is that students may not learn a comprehensive academic curriculum. For example, students might spend all of their time learning about science and never study any other basic subjects such as math or literature. I am also skeptical of whether homeschooled students can become properly socialized. Children need to interact with their peers. Homeschooled students spend most of their time with adults: their parents and tutors. They rarely have the chance to play with children their age. Due to this, homeschooled children may have difficulty adjusting into society as they grow older.

1 Underline the main idea of each opinion.

2 Which opinion is for the topic? Which one is against it?
- FOR: _____
- AGAINST: _____

3 What supporting ideas does each opinion give?
- Opinion A: _____
- Opinion B: _____

4 Create one more supporting idea for each argument.
- Opinion A: _____
- Opinion B: _____

Skills for Debate

Read and learn how to create expert opinion examples.

How Can You Create Expert Opinion Examples?

To make the most effective use of expert opinion examples, you must be sure to **make connections** between the **details** that you list from the expert opinion and your **argument**. After listing the relevant points from the expert opinion, you need to show how they apply directly to your argument. Do this by making **logical connections** between your example and argument. Use phrases such as "This is relevant to our point since…" and "This becomes clearer when we consider that…" to introduce your connections.

Practicing Debate Skills

Read the following arguments and expert examples and connections. Decide whether each connection is logical or illogical. If they are logical, explain why. If they are illogical, rewrite them to make them logical.

1 Homeschooled students have better academic achievement than traditional school students.

- **Example:** According to Princeton University Professor Sandra Clark, homeschooled students can excel academically because they are free from the distractions of learning at traditional schools. For instance, there are no problems relating to peer pressure or bullying in a homeschool environment.

- **Connection:** The relevance of this example is that students often have difficulty forming meaningful relationships at traditional schools, an issue which needs to be addressed before students' academic performance can improve. (LOGICAL/ILLOGICAL)

- **Explanation/Rewrite:** _____

2 Homeschooled children have difficulty socializing with their peers in later life.

- **Example:** Child psychologist Ethan Price believes that homeschooling denies children important opportunities to interact with people their age. As a result, these children often cannot relate to their peers and form lasting relationships with them once they enter adult society.

- **Connection:** We mention this because this shows the negative effects that being homeschooled has on a child's social development. (LOGICAL/ILLOGICAL)

- **Explanation/Rewrite:** _____

Unit 02 B Debating the Topic

Creating Your Debate

Motion: Homeschooling should be illegal.

What are your arguments? Get into two groups and plan for the debate. Decide whether your team is FOR (agree) or AGAINST (disagree) the motion. Then, create your ARE: Argument, Reason, and Example. Use the example arguments below and the research from your workbook to help create your arguments.

■ **Example Arguments**

FOR

Argument

Students may not learn enough by being homeschooled.

Reason

Unlike students at traditional schools, homeschooled students do not always learn from a professionally designed curriculum. A number of them simply study whatever their parents decide. The problem with this is that it is very likely for students to get an inadequate education.

Example

In one study of student achievement between homeschooled students and traditional school students, the homeschoolers performed much worse than traditional school students did. Their scores in reading and math ranged from 1 to 4 grade levels lower.

AGAINST

Argument

Homeschooling often enables students to excel academically.

Reason

Homeschooled students have more time and opportunities to pursue their academic interests than students in traditional schools have. This allows them to develop great academic skills while displaying a genuine understanding of their fields.

Example

Homeschooled student Jesse Orlowski was able to pursue his interests in math and science by taking college-level courses while he was still in high school. This helped him to surpass students at traditional high schools in these subjects.

Arguments FOR/AGAINST the Motion

ARGUMENT 1

Argument

Reason

Example

ARGUMENT 2

Argument

Reason

Example

ARGUMENT 3

Argument

Reason

Example

Actual Debate

Now, it's time to debate. Use the flow chart below to help you organize the debate.
The introductory expressions have been provided to help you. Put your arguments in logical order and make clear rebuttals to the opposing team's arguments.

Agree Opening Statement
That _____
_____
_____ is our team's main opinion.

Agree Argument 1
It must first be pointed out that _____
_____
_____
_____.

Rebuttal 1
You have it all wrong. Keep in mind that _____
_____
_____.

Agree Argument 2
Our next argument is _____
_____
_____.

Rebuttal 2
Your argument is flawed due to the fact that ___
_____
_____.

Agree Argument 3
Third, _____
_____
_____.

Agree Closing Statement
To us, there can be little doubt that _____
_____
_____.

Disagree Opening Statement
We, on the contrary, feel that _____
_____
_____.

Rebuttal 1
That is completely mistaken because _____
_____.

Disagree Argument 1
As for our first argument, it is that _____
_____
_____.

Rebuttal 2
Your reasoning that _____
_____ makes no sense because
_____.

Disagree Argument 2
Second, we posit that _____
_____.

Rebuttal 3
While you claim that _____
_____, we feel that
_____.

Disagree Argument 3
Our closing argument is _____
_____.

Disagree Closing Statement
Our firm conviction remains that _____
_____.

Sum Up the Debate

Finish the debate summary.

AGREEING SIDE'S ARGUMENT

_____ was our debate topic for today.

The opinion that _____ was given by the first team.

First, they said that _____.

To go into more detail, _____
_____.

They continued by mentioning that _____.

For example, _____
_____.

To conclude, the team pointed out that _____.

Their supporting evidence was _____
_____.

DISAGREEING SIDE'S ARGUMENT

The second team disagreed with the topic and claimed that _____
_____.

Their opening argument was _____
_____
_____ was their reasoning.

Next, they claimed that _____.

The details they provided were _____
_____.

The argument they gave last was _____.

Particularly, they mentioned that _____
_____.

Chapter 2

Creating Statistical Examples

Unit 03 Cutting CEO Salaries

Unit 04 Free Internet Service for the Poor

Unit 03 Cutting CEO Salaries

A. Discuss the following questions as a class.
1. What do you see in the picture above?
2. What do you think the man's job is? Why do you think so?
3. Does the man in the picture look generous or greedy to you? Explain.

B. Answer the following questions with a partner.
1. How much money do you think CEOs of large companies earn each year? How much money do you think they should be paid?
2. Why do you think companies pay CEOs such high salaries?
3. Do you think that paying CEOs less money would affect their job performance? Why or why not?

Unit 03 A Learning about the Topic

Should salaries for CEOs of large companies be cut?

Read the passage and underline the main ideas.

 Track 07

In 2013, the average annual salary of a CEO at an S&P 500 company was $11.7 million. This was 331 times greater than the typical pay for an American worker. By comparison, the median CEO salary in 1983 was $685,000, just 46 times greater than the earnings of a regular employee at the time. Despite the poor global financial situation, many CEOs keep getting pay raises. This situation is clearly **unmerited** for several reasons.

As it stands, most observers agree that CEOs are overpaid. For one, the salaries for CEOs have risen drastically faster than the pay for average workers has. Since 1983, CEOs in the United States have seen their incomes rise by 900 percent while normal workers have only had a pay increase of 10 percent. In addition, many CEOs purposely cut jobs in their home countries to save money. For decades, American companies have **outsourced** production to less developed nations where wages are low. This has enabled companies to increase their profit margins, which a number of CEOs have used to boost their own salaries. Worst of all, unprofitable companies continue to pay their CEOs millions of dollars a year. Several major multinational companies, such as General Motors, needed government **bailouts** to avoid bankruptcy. Despite their precarious financial situations, these conglomerates continued to compensate their CEOs with multimillion-dollar salaries and bonuses.

There are several reasons to justify the high pay of CEOs. The first is that CEOs help to expand their companies and to increase their profits. The main roles of CEOs are to **streamline** their companies' business models and to make them more competitive in order to be more profitable. When CEOs succeed in doing this, it is only logical to reward them with high salaries. CEOs should also make multimillion-dollar salaries since they have developed highly specialized sets of skills. Effective CEOs must understand their industries with great depth, know how to organize huge companies efficiently, and motivate their employees to do their best. This **distinct** blend of talents should be rewarded with exceptionally high salaries. Finally, CEOs have a huge responsibility. If CEOs do their jobs badly, then their companies can go bankrupt, and thousands of people can lose their jobs. This heavy burden must be compensated with an appropriately high salary.

Vocabulary Check

Choose the correct word for each definition.

| unmerited | outsource | bailout | streamline | distinct |

1. to make something more effective or productive _____
2. to send a company's work to be done by other people _____
3. the act of saving a business from money problems _____
4. not reasonable or proper _____
5. noticeably different _____

Comprehension Questions

Check the correct answer for each question.

1. How many years would an average American employee in 2013 have to work to earn a CEO's annual income?
   - ☐ 10
   - ☐ 46
   - ☐ 331
   - ☐ 900

2. Why do many CEOs outsource production to other countries according to the passage?
   - ☐ To reduce their companies' production costs to increase their salaries
   - ☐ To provide more job opportunities for people in less developed nations

3. What is the main job function of CEOs?
   - ☐ They work to obtain government bailouts so their companies can avoid bankruptcy.
   - ☐ They improve their companies' business models to make them more competitive.

4. Why does the passage mention the fact that people can lose their jobs?
   - ☐ To point out that the position of CEO requires great responsibility
   - ☐ To mention that CEOs care only about boosting their own incomes

Questions for Debate

Think of and share ideas to explore the debatable issues in the article. Be sure to state your opinion clearly and to provide one supporting idea for each opinion.

1. What do you think is an appropriate salary for a CEO? Explain.

   From my perspective, it is clear that _____
   _____.

   To go into more detail, _____
   _____.

2. Do you think that CEOs in your country are paid too much, too little, or just the right amount of money? Why?

   I feel that _____
   _____.

   The reason I feel this way is _____
   _____.

3. Is it right to continue paying huge salaries to CEOs when their companies are not profitable?

   It is my firm belief that _____
   _____.

   What I mean by this is _____
   _____.

4. What special talents or skills do CEOs have that most workers do not have?

   Most CEOs have _____
   _____.

   It is necessary to keep this in mind because _____
   _____.

5. Do you think companies could still be successful even if they paid their CEOs less money? Why or why not?

   I think that _____
   _____.

   This is due to the fact that _____
   _____.

Opinion Examples

Look at the opinion examples about the motion below and answer the questions.

> **Motion: CEOs are overpaid and should have their salaries reduced.**

Opinion A Track 08

There is no justifiable reason for CEOs to earn over 11 million dollars a year. Executive salaries must be cut immediately. One, consider the fact that executive pay has risen far faster than the average worker's pay: 900 percent versus the much smaller 10-percent pay increase the average worker received. This has not happened because CEOs have contributed much more to the economy; rather, it is the result of their manipulation of the market. This fact becomes even more disturbing when you consider that CEOs are often responsible for cutting the jobs of honest, hardworking people. In many companies, CEOs try to outsource as much work as possible so they can boost profits to increase their own incomes.

Opinion B Track 09

CEOs may earn incredibly high salaries, but it is for a good reason. CEOs have unique sets of skills and deserve high compensation. First of all, becoming a CEO of a huge company is extremely difficult. Only businesspeople with years of experience, knowledge, and business skills can be put into these positions. Their hard work and talents should be justly rewarded. Moreover, CEOs generate lots of income for their companies. Successful CEOs can help their companies to earn millions or even billions of dollars a year. Since CEOs are paid largely in the company stock they own, it is only reasonable for them to make millions of dollars when their companies do well.

1 Underline the main idea of each opinion.

2 Which opinion is for the topic? Which one is against it?
- FOR: _____
- AGAINST: _____

3 What supporting ideas does each opinion give?
- Opinion A: _____
- Opinion B: _____

4 Create one more supporting idea for each argument.
- Opinion A: _____
- Opinion B: _____

Skills for Debate

Read and learn how to create statistical examples.

How Can You Create Statistical Examples?

Another excellent example type is **statistical examples**. This is information in the form of **numbers** and **percentages**. Statistics are useful because they provide **clear, easy-to-understand evidence** in support of your argument. To help you accomplish this, you must first be able to select the data that most **strongly relates** to your argument. Focus on statistics where the **majority** or an **unusually high number** of incidents that support your argument occur. Then, explain the **meaning** of the statistic and its **relevance** to your argument. Be sure to use clear **transitions** such as "One statistic shows that…"

Practicing Debate Skills

Read the following argument and statistics. Use the information to create a statistical example. Define the statistic and explain the important data. Some information has been provided to help you.

- **Argument:** The rise in CEO salaries is unfair compared to the rise in average workers' salaries.

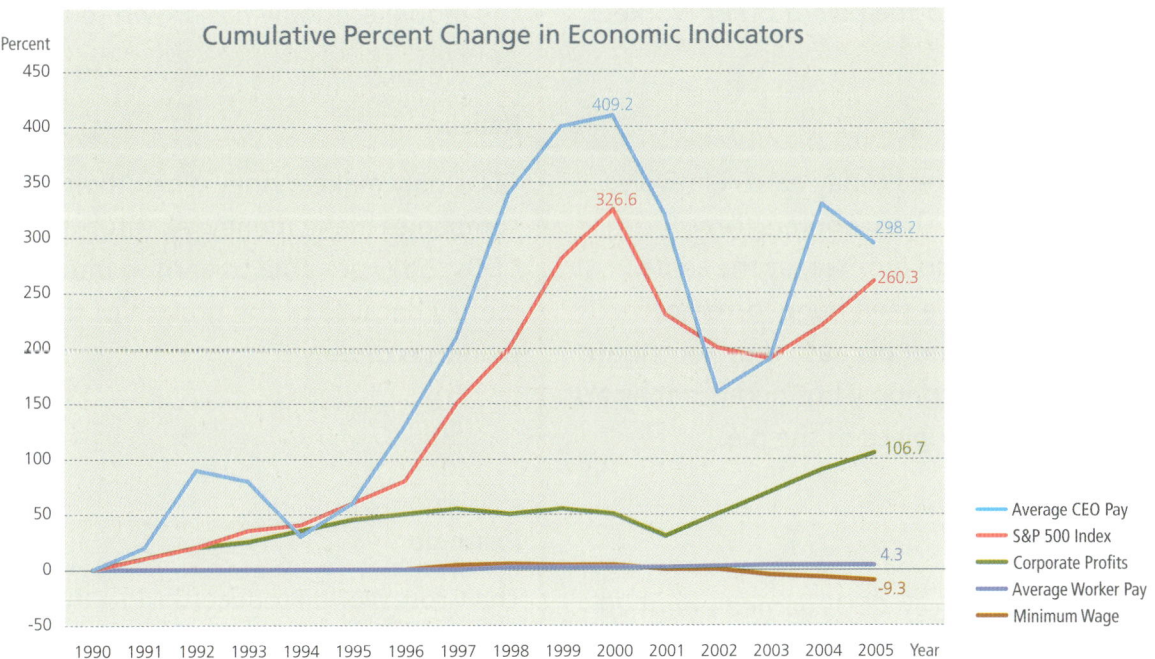

- **Example:** According to one study, the salary of CEOs rose by 409.2% in the year 2000. During the same year, the average worker pay and minimum wage both rose by _____. This clearly relates to our argument since _____
_____.

Unit 03 B Debating the Topic

Creating Your Debate

Motion: CEOs are overpaid and should have their salaries reduced.

What are your arguments? Get into two groups and plan for the debate. Decide whether your team is FOR (agree) or AGAINST (disagree) the motion. Then, create your ARE: Argument, Reason, and Example. Use the example arguments below and the research from your workbook to help create your arguments.

■ **Example Arguments**

FOR

Argument

CEO pay has risen much faster than the rate of inflation and the pay of other workers.

Reason

Nearly all workers today earn relatively higher salaries than workers three generations ago did. Yet, at the same time, CEOs have seen huge increases in their incomes not because they contribute more to the economy but because they are taking a larger piece of the pie.

Example

In 1965, American CEOs earned about 20 times more than their workers. By 1990, the rate had tripled to 60 times more. Today, CEOs earn roughly 300 times more than the average employee.

AGAINST

Argument

CEOs earn so much money today because the global economy has grown so large.

Reason

CEOs only make money when their companies make money. As it turns out, CEOs today are able to earn so much money because of the growth of the world's economy.

Example

The Gross World Product (GWP)—the total value of all goods and services produced each year in the entire world—was just 6.8 trillion dollars in 1960. Today, the GWP is over 75 trillion dollars. Since the GWP today is over 10 times greater, then it makes sense for CEOs' salaries to be 10 times greater, too.

Arguments FOR/AGAINST the Motion

ARGUMENT 1

Argument

_____
_____
_____
_____
_____
_____

Reason

_____
_____
_____
_____
_____
_____

Example

_____
_____
_____
_____
_____
_____

ARGUMENT 2

Argument

_____
_____
_____
_____
_____
_____

Reason

_____
_____
_____
_____
_____
_____

Example

_____
_____
_____
_____
_____
_____

ARGUMENT 3

Argument

_____
_____
_____
_____
_____
_____

Reason

_____
_____
_____
_____
_____
_____

Example

_____
_____
_____
_____
_____
_____

Actual Debate

Now, it's time to debate. Use the flow chart below to help you organize the debate.
The introductory expressions have been provided to help you. Put your arguments in logical order and make clear rebuttals to the opposing team's arguments.

Agree Opening Statement
We are convinced that _____.

Disagree Opening Statement
Our position, on the other hand, is that _____.

Agree Argument 1
To start off with, _____.

Rebuttal 1
We disagree. To us, it seems that _____.

Disagree Argument 1
As for our opening argument, it is _____.

Rebuttal 1
While our opponents claim that _____, we believe that _____.

Rebuttal 2
We are sorry, but we cannot agree because _____.

Agree Argument 2
We must also mention that _____.

Disagree Argument 2
Our next point is that _____.

Rebuttal 2
The problem with your argument is _____.

Rebuttal 3
The argument that _____ is incorrect since _____.

Agree Argument 3
Finally, _____.

Disagree Argument 3
To share our last point, _____.

Agree Closing Statement
In summary, _____.

Disagree Closing Statement
Our team remains sure that _____.

Sum Up the Debate

Finish the debate summary.

AGREEING SIDE'S ARGUMENT

The focus of our debate today was _____.

The first team agreed with the topic and stated that _____.

For starters, _____.

The supporting reason they gave was _____
_____.

Their second argument was _____.

This was illustrated by _____
_____.

To wrap up, they mentioned that _____.

For instance, _____
_____.

DISAGREEING SIDE'S ARGUMENT

On the contrary, the other team felt that _____
_____.

The first argument they mentioned was _____.

To be more specific, _____
_____.

Next, _____
_____
_____ was their detail.

Their closing argument was that _____.

Specifically, _____
_____.

Unit 04
Free Internet Service for the Poor

WARM-UP

A. Discuss the following questions as a class.

1. What do you see in the picture above?
2. What do you think the people are doing on the computer?
3. Do you think that these people have used the Internet much before? Why or why not?

B. Answer the following questions with a partner.

1. Does your government offer people free Internet access? If so, how can you use it?
2. Why is having Internet access so important in today's society?
3. Do you think the government should be responsible for providing free Internet service? Explain.

Unit 04 A Learning about the Topic

Should governments provide low-income citizens with free Internet service?

Read the passage and underline the main ideas.  Track 10

As of 2013, around 39 percent of people in the world had Internet access. In developed countries such as the United States, France, Germany, and South Korea, Internet **penetration** exceeds 80 percent. This statistic illustrates the significance of being online in today's world. Having Internet access opens up a world of information. Ironically, the people who would most benefit from using the Internet—the poor—often cannot afford to do so. This could be **rectified** if governments provide their low-income citizens with free Internet service in their homes.

The primary advantage of giving the poor free Internet service is that it would give them much greater access to information. For people to succeed in our society today, they must have specialized knowledge and training. Having free Internet access makes it possible for people to take online courses and to find jobs, both of which can **appreciably** boost their incomes and improve their quality of life. Along the same line of reasoning, giving the poor access to the Internet would make them more integrated into society. They would be able to use services such as email and social networking sites. This would allow them to connect with family members, friends, and people in their communities. It must also be pointed out that governments already provide numerous services for the poor, such as **subsidized** housing, food stamps, and daycare services. Providing free Internet would simply be another such service that the government would offer for the poor.

Even so, there is no **assurance** that having free Internet access will improve the lives of the poor. For one, Internet access could make the poor less economically productive. They can be easily tempted to spend all day watching videos or reading web comics than to take online classes or to apply for jobs. Next, it is unnecessary for governments to provide people with free Internet access. Most libraries, schools, and universities offer free Internet access for nearly everyone. This means that providing free Internet service would be a waste of government money and resources. Finally, having Internet access is a luxury, not a necessity. The government only has a responsibility to provide people with services that they need to survive. While having Internet access is beneficial, it is not as important as having food, water, and shelter, all of which governments must focus on providing for every citizen.

Vocabulary Check

Choose the correct word for each definition.

> penetration   rectify   appreciably   subsidized   assurance

1 to correct something that is wrong   _____
2 the act of going through or into something   _____
3 the state of being certain about something   _____
4 given money to help pay the cost of something   _____
5 by a noticeable or significant degree   _____

Comprehension Questions

Check the correct answer for each question.

1 How can having Internet access allow the poor to improve their quality of life?
   ☐ They can get jobs that allow them to work from home.
   ☐ They can take job-training courses over the Internet.

2 What are other services governments already provide for the poor? Choose TWO correct answers.

   ☐ kindergarten classes   ☐ food stamps
   ☐ subsidized housing   ☐ job training

3 Why would Internet access decrease poor people's economic productivity?
   ☐ Because they would no longer access the Internet at libraries and universities
   ☐ Because they could spend much of their time watching videos or reading comics

4 How would giving Internet access to the poor be a misuse of a government's budget?
   ☐ It is a service that it already available to citizens for free.
   ☐ It would take money away from other government services.

Questions for Debate

Think of and share ideas to explore the debatable issues in the article. Be sure to state your opinion clearly and to provide one supporting idea for each opinion.

1. Do you think it is important to have Internet access in today's society? Explain.

   From my point of view, it seems that _____
   _____.

   Allow me to explain by mentioning that _____
   _____.

2. How could having free Internet access allow low-income people to improve their quality of life?

   It would enable them to _____
   _____.

   What I mean by this is _____
   _____.

3. How could having free Internet access cause low-income people to decrease their productivity?

   There is a great chance that _____
   _____.

   This would be a problem because _____
   _____.

4. Many libraries and schools offer free Internet access to the public. Does this make offering free Internet access to people in their homes unnecessary?

   To me, it seems that _____
   _____.

   More specifically, _____
   _____.

5. Is it necessary for the government to provide low-income citizens with assistive services such as subsidized housing? Why or why not?

   I think the government should _____
   _____.

   This is due to the fact that _____
   _____.

Opinion Examples

Look at the opinion examples about the motion below and answer the questions.

> **Motion: The government should provide free Internet access to low-income citizens.**

Opinion A Track 11

It is crucial today for people to have access to the Internet to reach their potential. This is why the government should provide the poor with the Internet for free. Consider how people today find work. For a lot of people, getting a new job means going online to search job portal sites. Without reliable Internet access, the poor would lose this means of finding good high-paying jobs, which would make it even more difficult for them to earn enough money to survive. What's more, offering free Internet service would not cost much money. The infrastructure for the Internet—phone lines, satellites, and wires—is already in place. It would simply be a matter of connecting people's homes to this already-existing network.

Opinion B Track 12

The government should provide poor people with housing and food subsidies. What it does not need to subsidize is Internet access. Principally, having access to the Internet is not necessary. It is not needed to apply for jobs, to get an education, or to have entertainment. In other words, having the Internet is a luxury, so the government does not need to provide it. We also need to remember that there are already several ways for the poor to get online for free. Libraries, schools, and universities already offer no-cost Internet access for nearly everyone. This means that providing people with free Internet access would just be throwing away government money.

1 Underline the main idea of each opinion.

2 Which opinion is for the topic? Which one is against it?
- FOR: _____
- AGAINST: _____

3 What supporting ideas does each opinion give?
- Opinion A: _____
- Opinion B: _____

4 Create one more supporting idea for each argument.
- Opinion A: _____
- Opinion B: _____

Skills for Debate

Read and learn how to create statistical examples.

How Can You Create Statistical Examples?

As explained in the previous unit, you can use statistics to prove your arguments. However, you must also remember that statistics can be used to **disprove your opponents' arguments**. First, point out how your statistics support your argument. Then, mention how the same statistics make your **opponent's argument invalid**. You must be sure, though, that you **fully understand** your statistics and are sure that they **relate** to both **your argument** and your **opponent's argument**. Otherwise, the other team can exploit this flaw and make a strong rebuttal against you.

Practicing Debate Skills

Read the following argument and statistics. Use the provided information to explain the relevance of the statistic to your argument and how it disproves your opponent's argument. Some words have been provided to help you.

- **Argument:** The poor cannot afford to pay for Internet access.

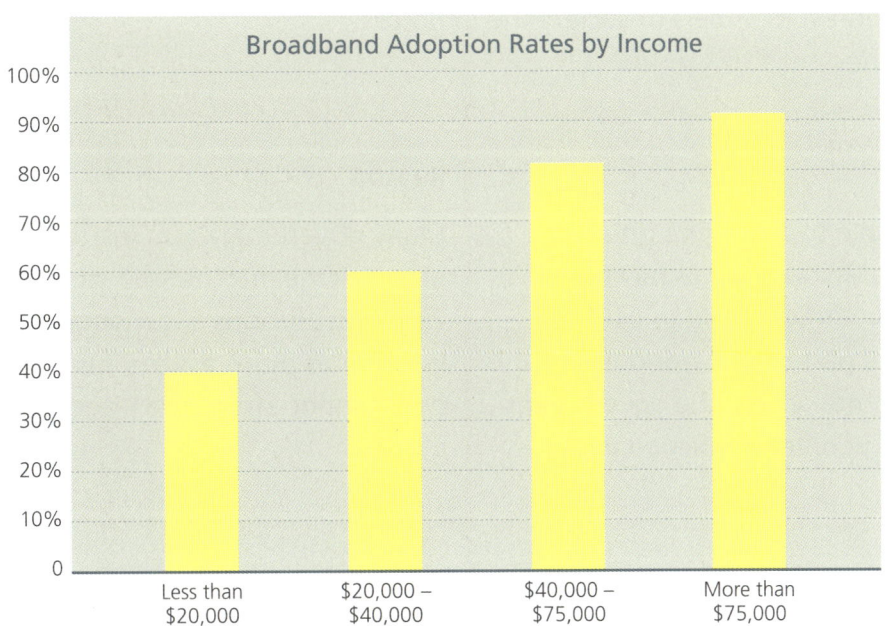

- **Example:** A study conducted by the Federal Communications Commission found that only 40 percent of households with incomes of less than $20,000 a year had broadband access in their homes. This is strongly related to our argument since _____. At the same time, this disproves our opponent's stance since _____.

Unit 04 B Debating the Topic

Creating Your Debate

Motion: The government should provide free Internet access to low-income citizens

What are your arguments? Get into two groups and plan for the debate. Decide whether your team is FOR (agree) or AGAINST (disagree) the motion. Then, create your ARE: Argument, Reason, and Example. Use the example arguments below and the research from your workbook to help create your arguments.

■ **Example Arguments**

FOR

Argument

The government has a responsibility to provide the poorest members of society the services that they need to survive.

Reason

While being able to access the Internet is not as crucial for survival as having a place to live or enough food to eat, it is still an integral part of our world today. By providing Internet access, the government can help poor people to function in our society.

Example

Specifically, having Internet access would allow the poor to find jobs, to continue their education, and to save money by giving them nearly unlimited access to information.

AGAINST

Argument

The poor can already access the Internet at no cost.

Reason

Many government-run institutions already provide free Internet service for citizens. These institutions allow people to use the Internet as much as they need to even if they cannot afford the Internet themselves.

Example

Nearly all public libraries in even middle-income countries provide citizens with free Internet access. This means that governments do not have to spend money unnecessarily on providing people with free Internet access in their homes.

Arguments FOR/AGAINST the Motion

ARGUMENT 1	ARGUMENT 2	ARGUMENT 3
Argument	**Argument**	**Argument**
Reason	**Reason**	**Reason**
Example	**Example**	**Example**

Actual Debate

Now, it's time to debate. Use the flow chart below to help you organize the debate.
The introductory expressions have been provided to help you. Put your arguments in logical order and make clear rebuttals to the opposing team's arguments.

Agree Opening Statement
From our point of view, there is no doubt that _____ .

Disagree Opening Statement
We feel the exact opposite. We are sure that _____ .

Agree Argument 1
For one, _____ .

Rebuttal 1
The problem with your argument that _____ is _____ .

Disagree Argument 1
First of all, _____ .

Rebuttal 1
That is simply not true since _____ .

Agree Argument 2
The second reason we will present is _____ .

Rebuttal 2
Unfortunately, you are still wrong because _____ .

Disagree Argument 2
We also contend that _____ .

Rebuttal 2
You claim that _____ , yet we feel that _____ .

Agree Argument 3
Finally, _____ .

Rebuttal 3
We are sorry, but we cannot agree. We are sure that _____ .

Disagree Argument 3
Our last argument is _____ .

Agree Closing Statement
The idea that _____ remains our overall opinion.

Disagree Closing Statement
To restate, our feeling is _____ .

Sum Up the Debate

Finish the debate summary.

AGREEING SIDE'S ARGUMENT

The topic of today's debate was _____.

_____ was the first team's opinion.

For starters, they claimed that _____.

To give their example, _____
_____.

Their next point was _____.

This was supported by _____
_____.

Lastly, they posited that _____
_____.

_____ was their evidence.

DISAGREEING SIDE'S ARGUMENT

Meanwhile, the other team argued that _____
_____.

First, they stated that _____.

For instance, _____
_____.

The next argument they made was _____.

In detail, _____
_____.

Finally, _____.

This was strengthened by the notion that _____
_____.

Chapter 3

Creating Academic Studies Examples

Unit 05 Extending the School Year

Unit 06 Detaining the Mentally Ill

Unit 05 Extending the School Year

A. Discuss the following questions as a class.
1. What do you see in the picture above?
2. Why do you think this girl is tired?
3. How many hours a day would the girl need in order to study all of her books?

B. Answer the following questions with a partner.
1. How many days a year do you go to school? Do you think that this is an appropriate amount?
2. Do you think that longer school years improve students' academic performances? Explain.
3. What are some activities that students should do that do not involve studying?

Unit 05 A Learning about the Topic

Should school years be extended to help students learn more?

Read the passage and underline the main ideas. Track 13

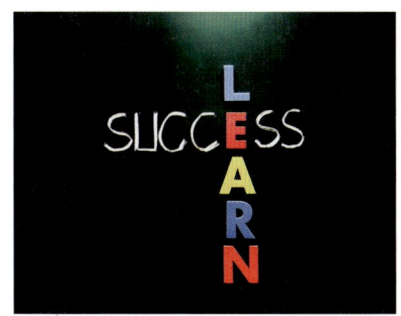

U.S. President Barack Obama once criticized the American school system for insufficiently educating students. One of his main arguments was that American students do not spend enough time in the classroom each year. He pointed out that South Korean students spend more than 220 days a year in school and **boast** some of the highest test scores in the world while American students are in school a **paltry** 180 days annually and have below-average academic performance. Does President Obama have the right idea? Would extending the school year allow students to learn more?

Much evidence suggests the president is right. When students spend more time in school—either by going to school for more days each year or by having longer school days—their academic performance improves. The reason is that students need to spend more time in class to absorb and retain greater amounts of information. Likewise, longer school years would give teachers more **flexibility** to cover the subjects that are the most difficult for students. At KIPP Academy in the United States—a government-sponsored magnet school—students spend three times longer learning math and science than do students at public schools. Consequently, their test scores in these subjects are twice as high on average. Finally, longer school years would **stimulate** a culture of learning. Students would feel a greater connection with their teachers and fellow classmates by having longer school days.

There are still problems with extending the school year. The first problem is funding. Education is underfunded in many countries, and school districts cannot afford to pay teachers higher salaries for working longer hours. Another concern is that spending more time in school may not automatically lead to better academic performance. Students who have longer school years do not always get higher grades. What is more important is the amount of effort students put into their studies and the **efficacy** of their study programs. Lengthening the school year can also put an emotional strain on students. If children spend more time in school, they will have fewer chances to socialize with their friends, which will make them more stressed and less happy. One study found that children in South Korea are among the least happy in the world largely because they have one of the longest school years of any nation.

Vocabulary Check

Choose the correct word for each definition.

| boast | paltry | flexibility | stimulate | efficacy |

1 to make something more active _____
2 to have something that is impressive _____
3 the state of being able to be changed _____
4 the power to produce a desired result _____
5 very small or too small in amount _____

Comprehension Questions

Check the correct answer for each question.

1 Why did President Obama mention South Korea in his argument about education?
 ☐ To point out a country where students have superior academic performance
 ☐ To mention an example of a nation that recently made its school year longer

2 How does KIPP Academy help students to do better at math and science?
 ☐ By forcing students to study during their winter and summer vacations
 ☐ By tripling the amount of time that students spend studying these subjects

3 What is the main problem in extending the school year regarding teachers?
 ☐ They may not be able to help students get better grades.
 ☐ They cannot be given extra money to work longer hours.

4 How would extending the school year affect students?
 ☐ Students would not have enough time to relax and to play with their friends.
 ☐ Students would put less effort into their studies and become more tired.

Questions for Debate

Think of and share ideas to explore the debatable issues in the article. Be sure to state your opinion clearly and to provide one supporting idea for each opinion.

1. How long is the school year in your country? Do you think the school year is too long, too short, or an appropriate length? Explain.

   In my country, the school year is _____
   _____.

   I think that this length is _____
   _____.

2. Will making the school year longer automatically improve students' academic performances? Why or why not?

   From my point of view, it is clear that _____
   _____.

   I feel this way due to the fact that _____
   _____.

3. Do you think that teachers would support making the school year longer? Explain.

   It is most likely that _____
   _____.

   This is important to keep in mind because _____
   _____.

4. What difficulties would a longer school year present for school districts themselves?

   If the school year were made longer, then _____
   _____.

   In more detail, _____
   _____.

5. Aside from making the school year longer, what are some ways that a country can improve the academic performances of its students?

   Some possible alternatives include _____
   _____.

   The reason I think that these would be better is _____
   _____.

Opinion Examples

Look at the opinion examples about the motion below and answer the questions.

> **Motion: The school year should be made longer to enable students to learn more.**

Opinion A Track 14

I'm an American middle school student, and I go to school just 180 days out of the year. Some students in other countries might be jealous of me, but they have no reason to be. The longer the school year is, the better. The biggest problem is that our summer break is too long. It lasts over three months. By the time I go back to school, I've already forgotten most of what I learned in the previous grade. A longer school year would also make it easier to master tricky subjects. Many students at my school struggle with math and science because we only study these subjects one hour a day. With a longer school year, then we could easily double or triple the amount of time we spend learning these subjects.

Opinion B Track 15

Students already spend enough time in school. Extending the school year will not boost students' performance; improving the education system will. For starters, students won't learn more just by spending more time in school. The quality of their classes matters more. To help students learn more, governments need to make sure that their teachers are well qualified and trained to teach their subjects. Similarly, students must be motivated to learn. Even if the school year were 250 days long, students may not learn very much if they have no desire to improve themselves. Therefore, schools need to work on teaching their students to value education and show them how studying hard will lead to success later on.

1 Underline the main idea of each opinion.

2 Which opinion is for the topic? Which one is against it?
- FOR: _____
- AGAINST: _____

3 What supporting ideas does each opinion give?
- Opinion A: _____
- Opinion B: _____

4 Create one more supporting idea for each argument.
- Opinion A: _____
- Opinion B: _____

Skills for Debate

Read and learn how to create academic studies examples.

How Can You Create Academic Studies Examples?

Academic studies examples use research done by university professors, government researchers, and researchers at commercial organizations. The findings of academic studies are usually the result of several tests conducted on a large number of people. They are an excellent way to support your argument. First, mention **who created the study** by using a phrase such as "According to a study conducted by…" Then, state the **purpose of the study**. "The main goal of the study was…" is a good phrase to do this. Finally, mention the **findings which relate** to your argument, and introduce them with a phrase like "This directly supports our argument that…"

Practicing Debate Skills

Read the following academic study article. Underline the relevant information you wish to include in your example. Then, use the phrases provided to create your example. Be sure to explain the relevance of it.

- **Academic Study – Georgetown University Professors Joseph Goldberg and William Nimitz**

  The recent push to extend the length of the school day in the United States has met with a lot of criticism from both parents and teachers. Nevertheless, our research on the Washington, D.C. KIPP charter schools provides compelling evidence in favor of a longer school day. At KIPP, students spend 60 percent more time in school than students in traditional schools do. They go from 7:30 a.m. to 5 p.m. from Monday to Friday and take some Saturday classes. Consequently, the students at KIPP outperform students at regular public schools in every measure. In 2010, 89 percent of eighth-grade students tested proficient or above in math compared to the D.C. average of 27 percent. In reading, 81 percent of KIPP students scored proficient while D.C. students as a whole scored 32 percent. Even more impressive, nearly four-fifths of KIPP students attend college, which is far greater than the one-fifth average for students in the capital. We have concluded that the superior performance of KIPP students is a direct result of spending more time in the classroom. Teachers at KIPP can cover topics in more depth and assist students who are struggling. We therefore recommend that all schools adopt a longer school day.

- **Example:** A recent study conducted by _____
  found that students who _____
  have better _____. To conduct
  their research, the professors examined _____
  located in Washington, D.C. Their findings were clear: The longer school day at KIPP
  allowed students to _____. Specifically, _____
  _____. This is relevant to our argument since _____
  _____.

Unit 05 B Debating the Topic

Creating Your Debate

Motion: The school year should be made longer to enable students to learn more.

What are your arguments? Get into two groups and plan for the debate. Decide whether your team is FOR (agree) or AGAINST (disagree) the motion. Then, create your ARE: Argument, Reason, and Example. Use the example arguments below and the research from your workbook to help create your arguments.

■ **Example Arguments**

FOR

Argument

Students who spend more time in school have better academic performance.

Reason

Developing any skill—whether it is playing the violin or learning about world history—requires a major time investment. The more time people devote to learning a skill, the better they will become at it. By making the school year longer, students will have more chances to develop their academic skills and knowledge.

Example

For example, South Korea has the longest school year of any country in the world at 220 days. Not surprisingly, the nation's students have some of the best academic performance in the world.

AGAINST

Argument

A longer school year does not guarantee better academic performance.

Reason

A longer school year does not improve education; better teachers and class materials as well as a culture of learning do. In an ineffective academic program, students may spend a lot of time at school yet learn very little.

Example

In Mexico, the school year is 200 days long. It is the second longest in the world. Despite this, Mexican students have academic performance far below the global average. This is due to the fact that Mexican schools and teachers do not provide a quality education.

■ Arguments FOR/AGAINST the Motion

ARGUMENT 1

Argument

_____
_____
_____
_____
_____
_____

Reason

_____
_____
_____
_____
_____
_____

Example

_____
_____
_____
_____
_____
_____

ARGUMENT 2

Argument

_____
_____
_____
_____
_____
_____

Reason

_____
_____
_____
_____
_____
_____

Example

_____
_____
_____
_____
_____
_____

ARGUMENT 3

Argument

_____
_____
_____
_____
_____
_____

Reason

_____
_____
_____
_____
_____
_____

Example

_____
_____
_____
_____
_____
_____

Actual Debate

Now, it's time to debate. Use the flow chart below to help you organize the debate.
The introductory expressions have been provided to help you. Put your arguments in logical order and make clear rebuttals to the opposing team's arguments.

Agree Opening Statement
We strongly believe that _____.

Disagree Opening Statement
We feel otherwise. It is our conviction that _____.

Rebuttal 1
While our opponents think that _____, we must point out that _____.

Agree Argument 1
Most of all, _____.

Disagree Argument 1
As for our first point, it is _____.

Rebuttal 1
What you have failed to realize is _____.

Rebuttal 2
Even though you feel that _____, it is necessary to keep in mind that _____.

Agree Argument 2
Second, consider that _____.

Disagree Argument 2
Next, _____.

Rebuttal 2
That is not true. The fact is that _____.

Rebuttal 3
Once again, you are mistaken. Remember that _____.

Agree Argument 3
As for our final argument, it is _____.

Disagree Argument 3
Lastly, we must bring up that _____.

Agree Closing Statement
Overall, we feel that _____.

Disagree Closing Statement
To us, there is no doubt that _____.

Sum Up the Debate

Finish the debate summary.

AGREEING SIDE'S ARGUMENT

The topic of today's debate was _____.

The first team's opinion was _____.

First, they stated that _____.

To be specific, _____
_____.

Their next argument was _____.

The evidence they offered as support was _____
_____.

The argument that they presented last was _____.

Their example was _____
_____.

DISAGREEING SIDE'S ARGUMENT

Conversely, it was the opinion of the second team that _____
_____.

For starters, they pointed out that _____.

They went into detail by explaining that _____
_____.

Second, they argued that _____.

The notion that _____
_____ was given to support their argument.

Their concluding argument was _____.

This was illustrated by _____
_____.

65

Unit 06 Detaining the Mentally Ill

WARM-UP

A. Discuss the following questions as a class.
1. What do you see in the picture above?
2. What do you think the people in the picture are talking about?
3. How do people with mental illnesses usually receive treatment?

B. Answer the following questions with a partner.
1. What are some common symptoms of mental illnesses?
2. Why are people suffering from mental illnesses less likely to receive appropriate treatment?
3. How can the mentally ill sometimes pose a danger to people in society?

Unit 06   A   Learning about the Topic

Should doctors be able to detain the mentally ill indefinitely?

Read the passage and underline the main ideas.    Track 16

Approximately 1 out of 17 people in the United States suffers from serious mental illnesses such as schizophrenia and bipolar disorder. People with these conditions can pose a danger to both themselves and the public. This is why doctors **confine** patients showing symptoms of a mental illness. Under current laws, the detention period is short—only 72 hours at most. To provide more effective treatment, some doctors are arguing for the right to detain patients with mental illnesses indefinitely.

Mandatory detention for the mentally ill would make sure that these patients receive proper medical care. Doctors would have the ability to detain these patients as long as necessary, thereby allowing them to provide more accurate **diagnoses** and better treatment. Second, it would keep the public safe. People suffering from schizophrenia and bipolar disorder have difficulty controlling their **impulses**, and this can make them more violent than mentally healthy individuals. A study by the *American Journal of Psychiatry* found that people with severe personality disorders committed around 10 percent of all homicides in the United States despite **comprising** only 3 percent of the population. A final point is that any detention bill would be in line with human rights. In 2007, the British Mental Health Act to confine mental patients was created in accordance with current human rights laws.

Some people fear that allowing indefinite detention periods for the mentally unhealthy would deter these people from seeking help. The reason is they would know that they could be held indefinitely as a result of their diagnoses. In one survey, 1 out of 3 people suffering from depression would avoid seeking treatment if they could be detained because of their condition. There is also little evidence to prove that people suffering from mental illnesses are more dangerous than the general population. Research shows that people under the influence of alcohol commit the majority of violent crimes and homicides—over 51 percent. The final point is that allowing doctors to detain people with mental illnesses could create a harmful **stigma** about people suffering from these disorders. People may come to believe wrongly that all mentally ill patients are threats to society when, in fact, the majority of them are not.

Vocabulary Check

Choose the correct word for each definition.

| confine | diagnosis | impulse | comprise | stigma |

1 to keep a person in a place _____

2 to be made up of something _____

3 a sudden strong desire to do something _____

4 the act of identifying a disease through examination _____

5 a set of unfair beliefs people have about something _____

Comprehension Questions

Check the correct answer for each question.

1 How would indefinite detention periods allow doctors to provide better treatment?
   - ☐ They could more accurately understand patients' symptoms.
   - ☐ They could diagnose undiscovered mental illnesses.

2 Why are the mentally ill more likely to be violent than healthy people?
   - ☐ Because they do not realize that they can be sent to prison
   - ☐ Because they cannot properly restrain their aggression

3 What is the reason that people would not seek treatment if indefinite detention periods were allowed?
   - ☐ They would not want to be detained if the doctor diagnoses them with a mental illness.
   - ☐ They would not have the right to receive treatment according to human rights laws.

4 Why does the passage mention that 51 percent of violent crimes are committed by people who are drunk?
   - ☐ To point out that alcohol makes it difficult for people to control their impulses
   - ☐ To suggest that the mentally ill are not especially violent or dangerous

Questions for Debate

Think of and share ideas to explore the debatable issues in the article. Be sure to state your opinion clearly and to provide one supporting idea for each opinion.

1 What are some problems that can occur if a person's mental illness goes untreated?

It is my feeling that _____

_____.

The reason that I believe this is _____

_____.

2 Why is it important for doctors to have the right to detain people with mental disorders?

Doctors should be able to detain these people since _____

_____.

For instance, _____

_____.

3 How is treating mental illnesses different from treating other medical conditions?

It is different in terms of _____

_____.

What I mean by this is _____

_____.

4 Should doctors be able to decide by themselves how long to detain patients, or should they have the consent of a patient's family first?

Most of the time, I think it would be better for _____

_____.

To be more specific, _____

_____.

5 Do you think allowing doctors to detain patients indefinitely will cause mentally ill people to seek treatment or to avoid it?

My opinion is that _____

_____.

Consider that _____

_____.

Opinion Examples

Look at the opinion examples about the motion below and answer the questions.

> **Motion: Doctors should be allowed to detain mentally ill patients indefinitely.**

Opinion A Track 17

It is true that the majority of people with mental illnesses do not receive proper treatment, but this does not mean that doctors should have the right to confine these people indefinitely. The main problem with this is that it gives doctors too much power. Such a law would allow one or two doctors to hold patients simply because they show symptoms of mental illnesses. This could lead to potentially dangerous situations of doctors detaining people without the consent of individuals or their families. Likewise, this law would discourage people from seeking treatment. Who would see a doctor to check whether he or she has a mental illness if that person might not be able to leave the doctor's custody?

Opinion B Track 18

There are several effective ways to treat mental illnesses today. Unfortunately, current laws do not give doctors enough power to do so. This is why the government must allow doctors to detain the mentally ill. People who suffer from personality disorders are often unaware of their condition. Even worse, some patients actively avoid getting treatment. If doctors could detain these patients, they could administer proper treatments more easily. Detainment laws would also keep the public safer. Studies show that the mentally ill commit violent crimes at a far greater rate than mentally healthy individuals. Detaining the mentally ill would keep them away from the public while enabling them to become healthy again.

1. Underline the main idea of each opinion.

2. Which opinion is for the topic? Which one is against it?
   - FOR: _____
   - AGAINST: _____

3. What supporting ideas does each opinion give?
   - Opinion A: _____
   - Opinion B: _____

4. Create one more supporting idea for each argument.
   - Opinion A: _____
   - Opinion B: _____

Skills for Debate

Read and learn how to create academic studies examples.

How Can You Create Academic Studies Examples?

When making academic studies examples, you have to be able to find and summarize the information that is the most relevant to your argument. You must not only determine which **information is relevant** to your point but also **paraphrase the information clearly**. To do this, you must use specific **nouns** and **verbs** central to the topic and your arguments. Be sure to explain exactly how your research proves your argument or disproves your opponent's argument.

Practicing Debate Skills

Read the excerpts from students' academic studies examples below. Decide whether the information they provide supports their arguments effectively or ineffectively. If their examples are effective, explain why. If they are ineffective, rewrite them to make them stronger.

1 Argument: The mentally ill pose a major threat to society and must be detained until they are cured.

   Example: According to one study, the most common violent crimes are armed robberies, home break-ins, and physical assaults. The best way to reduce the number of these crimes from occurring is to put their perpetrators in supervised care.

   Explanation: (EFFECTIVE/INEFFECTIVE) _____

   _____

   _____

2 Argument: The majority of people with mental illnesses do not receive adequate treatment.

   Example: Researchers at the London School of Medicine have determined that more than one-third of people with serious mental illnesses refuse to seek treatment. This is largely the result of their diseases, which cause them to believe mistakenly that they are mentally healthy.

   Explanation: (EFFECTIVE/INEFFECTIVE) _____

   _____

   _____

Unit 06 B Debating the Topic

Creating Your Debate

Motion: Doctors should be allowed to detain mentally ill patients indefinitely.

What are your arguments? Get into two groups and plan for the debate. Decide whether your team is FOR (agree) or AGAINST (disagree) the motion. Then, create your ARE: Argument, Reason, and Example. Use the example arguments below and the research from your workbook to help create your arguments.

■ **Example Arguments**

FOR

Argument

Treating mental illnesses properly requires doctors to examine patients for extended periods.

Reason

It is difficult to diagnose mental illnesses correctly. The symptoms of one disorder can initially appear similar to the symptoms from other disorders. To make an accurate assessment, doctors need to monitor patients for several days, weeks, or even months.

Example

According to the National Institute of Mental Health, around 85 percent of people with mental disorders meet the diagnostic measures for other mental illnesses. As a result, these patients often receive incorrect treatment.

AGAINST

Argument

Making mandatory detention laws for mental patients violates human rights laws.

Reason

The mentally ill are people, too. They have the right to personal freedom and liberties just like all other citizens do. However, when doctors are able to detain these patients without just cause, these patients lose their rights. They become treated like criminals even when they have done no wrong.

Example

While detaining mentally unstable individuals may be in the public's interest, these individuals should still have the right to decline treatment if they so desire.

■ Arguments FOR/AGAINST the Motion

ARGUMENT 1

Argument

_____
_____
_____
_____
_____
_____

Reason

_____
_____
_____
_____
_____
_____

Example

_____
_____
_____
_____
_____
_____

ARGUMENT 2

Argument

_____
_____
_____
_____
_____
_____

Reason

_____
_____
_____
_____
_____
_____

Example

_____
_____
_____
_____
_____
_____

ARGUMENT 3

Argument

_____
_____
_____
_____
_____
_____

Reason

_____
_____
_____
_____
_____
_____

Example

_____
_____
_____
_____
_____
_____

Actual Debate

Now, it's time to debate. Use the flow chart below to help you organize the debate.
The introductory expressions have been provided to help you. Put your arguments in logical order and make clear rebuttals to the opposing team's arguments.

Agree Opening Statement
Our team is positive that _____
_____.

Agree Argument 1
Our primary argument is _____
_____
_____
_____
_____
_____.

Rebuttal 1
What you say is not true since _____
_____.

Agree Argument 2
Furthermore, we contend that _____
_____
_____.

Rebuttal 2
Unlike the other team, it is our perspective
that _____
_____.

Agree Argument 3
We will finish by mentioning that _____
_____
_____.

Agree Closing Statement
To sum up, we strongly believe that _____
_____
_____
_____.

Disagree Opening Statement
We completely oppose the idea that _____
_____.

Rebuttal 1
Though our opponents claim that _____
_____, we believe that
_____.

Disagree Argument 1
The first point we will make is _____
_____.

Rebuttal 2
Despite your argument that _____
_____,
the truth of the matter is _____
_____.

Disagree Argument 2
It is also our belief that _____
_____.

Rebuttal 3
We refute the claim that _____
_____ because
_____.

Disagree Argument 3
Last, _____
_____.

Disagree Closing Statement
Our overall opinion is _____
_____.

Sum Up the Debate

Finish the debate summary.

AGREEING SIDE'S ARGUMENT

Our debate today dealt with the topic of _____.

The first team claimed that _____.

For starters, they argued that _____.

They explained that _____
_____.

They followed this with the notion that _____.

To share their example, _____
_____.

_____ was their closing argument.

Their evidence was _____
_____.

DISAGREEING SIDE'S ARGUMENT

To oppose the first team, the second team asserted that _____
_____.

They initially argued that _____.

For instance, _____
_____.

They then pointed out that _____
_____.

_____ was their main supporting reason.

Finally, they stated that _____.

To share their details, _____
_____.

75

Chapter 4

Creating Effective Rebuttals

Unit 07 Free Trade Agreements

Unit 08 Colonizing Other Planets

Unit 07 Free Trade Agreements

WARM-UP

A. Discuss the following questions as a class.

1. What do you see in the picture above?
2. Why do you think the two men in the picture are about to shake hands?
3. What countries' flags are in the picture? Why are they significant?

B. Answer the following questions with a partner.

1. Does your country have free trade agreements with other nations? If so, which ones?
2. How can a nation's consumers benefit from free trade agreements?
3. How can a nation's domestic companies suffer because of free trade agreements?

Unit 07 A Learning about the Topic

Should countries enact free trade agreements with other nations?

Read the passage and underline the main ideas. Track 19

Our global economy today is largely the result of multilateral free trade agreements (FTAs). These are voluntary agreements signed between two or more nations to trade their goods more freely by reducing or removing **tariffs**, quotas, and other protectionist measures. In theory, FTAs provide the most efficient **allocation** of resources and cheaper prices for consumers. In practice, these agreements often benefit only rich nations and their multinational corporations. In consideration of this, is it wise for countries to enact free trade agreements with other nations?

On the one hand, FTAs enable partner nations to trade their goods more cheaply. This encourages consumers in these nations to buy more products from the other nations in the agreement. For instance, the United States and South Korea have signed an FTA known as the KORUS FTA. The agreement is expected to boost the annual gross domestic product (GDP) of both economies by more than $10 billion. FTAs also promote efficiency through **specialization**. In economics, the idea that each nation can produce certain goods or items much more efficiently than other nations is known as comparative advantage. With FTAs, nations will produce only the goods they can make more cheaply than other nations. Most of all, consumers can enjoy a better quality of life. These trade agreements increase the number of products available in a country while making them cheaper to buy.

On the other hand, FTAs can unfairly disadvantage industries in many nations. The **provisions** of FTAs are rarely equal; mostly, richer nations get more advantages from FTAs. This weakens nations that already have underdeveloped economies. A related concern is how FTAs make it extremely difficult for smaller companies to compete with large multinational corporations. Huge international companies use FTAs to expand their businesses and to drive smaller foreign competitors into **bankruptcy**. This can lead to the disappearance of domestic companies and industries in smaller, less economically developed nations. Finally, FTAs harm the poor more than they help them. Free trade agreements provide companies with easier access to foreign labor markets. This allows companies to outsource their lower-skilled positions to countries where wages are cheaper. Because of this, millions of working-class laborers in wealthy nations end up losing their jobs and cannot find suitable replacement positions.

Vocabulary Check

Choose the correct word for each definition.

> tariff   allocation   specialization   provision   bankruptcy

1 the act of distributing something _____
2 a condition included as a part of an agreement _____
3 a situation of not having enough money to pay one's debts _____
4 a tax on goods entering or leaving a country _____
5 the act of limiting one's business to a single area or field _____

Comprehension Questions

Check the correct answer for each question.

1 What is an FTA according to the passage?
   ☐ An agreement to protect the domestic industries of a nation
   ☐ A deal between at least two countries to reduce trade barriers

2 Why do FTAs increase the GDPs of partner nations?
   ☐ Because they stimulate consumer spending due to lower prices on imported goods
   ☐ Because they encourage companies to develop new products for foreign customers

3 How do FTAs lead to comparative advantage?
   ☐ Consumers will enjoy having a greater number of foreign products available to purchase.
   ☐ Countries will produce only the goods that they can make more cheaply than other nations.

4 What effect do FTAs have on semi-skilled workers in advanced countries?
   ☐ They cause these workers to lose their jobs to laborers in other countries with lower wages.
   ☐ They make it difficult for these workers to find suitable replacement jobs in other industries.

Questions for Debate

Think of and share ideas to explore the debatable issues in the article. Be sure to state your opinion clearly and to provide one supporting idea for each opinion.

1 Which countries do you think that your nation should make FTAs with? Why?

It is my feeling that _____

_____.

I feel this way because _____

_____.

2 What are some reasons that a nation would want to make FTAs with other countries?

The primary reasons are _____

_____.

This is due to the fact that _____

_____.

3 How can FTAs benefit rich nations more than poor nations?

Rich nations are more likely to benefit because _____

_____.

To give a specific example, _____

_____.

4 Protectionist measures do not allow foreign companies to import their products into a nation. Do you think this situation is helpful or harmful to consumers?

My perspective on this issue is _____

_____.

For instance, _____

_____.

5 How can the enactment of FTAs lead to the economic dominance of only a small number of nations?

There is no doubt that _____

_____.

The reason for this is _____

_____.

Opinion Examples

Look at the opinion examples about the motion below and answer the questions.

Motion: Countries should enact free trade agreements with other nations.

Opinion A Track 20

My nation is a member of several free trade agreements, and I have seen the benefits they bring firsthand. Primarily, FTAs lead to lower prices. In some countries, tariffs increase the prices of goods by more than 50 percent. FTAs get rid of these tariffs, bringing about lower prices for consumers in the long term. A second advantage of FTAs is the fact that they lead to products of better quality. When nations become more open to foreign trade, it creates more competition for domestic firms. They are forced to improve the quality of their products or go bankrupt. Consumers again benefit by having more high-quality goods to choose from at lower prices.

Opinion B Track 21

Theoretically, FTAs sound like a great idea. Practically, they are not. Most of the time, FTAs are created between a rich nation and a poorer nation. Rich countries use these agreements to gain access to new foreign markets. Companies from these wealthy nations are able to produce their products more cheaply than companies from the poorer nations, which are then driven out of business. There is also not much evidence to suggest that FTAs actually lower prices. While tariffs may go down because of FTAs, companies usually keep their prices the same and pocket the difference. This means that the only ones saving money from FTAs are huge, rich companies.

1 Underline the main idea of each opinion.

2 Which opinion is for the topic? Which one is against it?
- FOR: _____
- AGAINST: _____

3 What supporting ideas does each opinion give?
- Opinion A: _____
- Opinion B: _____

4 Create one more supporting idea for each argument.
- Opinion A: _____
- Opinion B: _____

Skills for Debate

Read and learn how to create effective rebuttals.

How Can You Create Effective Rebuttals?

One of the most important debate skills is giving **rebuttals**. When you make rebuttals, you point out any **logical flaws**, **untrue statements**, or **irrelevant examples** in your opponents' arguments. To do this, you must **listen carefully** to the other team's arguments and **think critically** about them as you do so. After you determine the weakness of your opponents' ideas, you must then explain why their **arguments are wrong** and how it **weakens their overall position**.

Practicing Debate Skills

Read the argument below. Then, analyze the argument and answer the questions for making a rebuttal. Finally, use the answers that you come up with to make a rebuttal and to explain why the opposite argument is more persuasive.

- **Argument:** Free trade agreements lead to lower prices for consumers. Companies no longer have to pay high tariffs on the products they import, so they can reduce the prices of their products. This allows consumers to save money. For instance, South Korea recently made an FTA with the European Union. European products will become cheaper as a result.

Questions for Making a Rebuttal

1 Which parts of this argument are facts, and which parts are assumptions?
   _____

2 What flawed assumption does this argument make about the actions of companies?
   _____

3 Why is this example weak? What details is it missing?
   _____

- **Rebuttal:** The problem with the other team's argument is _____
  _____.

  To explain why, consider that _____
  _____.

Unit 07 B Debating the Topic

Creating Your Debate

Motion: Countries should enact free trade agreements with other nations.

What are your arguments? Get into two groups and plan for the debate. Decide whether your team is FOR (agree) or AGAINST (disagree) the motion. Then, create your ARE: Argument, Reason, and Example. Use the example arguments below and the research from your workbook to help create your arguments.

- **Example Arguments**

FOR

Argument

Free trade agreements lead to the most efficient allocation of resources.

Reason

Companies with closed economies often try to produce a huge variety of goods even when they lack the natural resources or knowhow to make them. This is a waste of time and labor. With FTAs, countries are forced to make only products that they can produce efficiently.

Example

For instance, Indonesia has huge amounts of natural resources such as wood. FTAs force the country to focus on its strengths—exporting natural resources—rather than wasting money on industries in which it cannot compete.

AGAINST

Argument

Free trade agreements unfairly benefit nations that are larger or already economically developed.

Reason

It is impossible for trade agreements between two nations to be fair. Larger or richer nations are always going to have advantages over their smaller trading partners. Signing FTAs can worsen the trade situations for smaller nations by giving wealthy nations even more advantages in trade.

Example

In 2000, Jordan signed an FTA with the United States. Today, domestic companies in Jordan struggle to compete with larger, more powerful American firms.

■ **Arguments FOR/AGAINST the Motion**

ARGUMENT 1	ARGUMENT 2	ARGUMENT 3
Argument	**Argument**	**Argument**
Reason	**Reason**	**Reason**
Example	**Example**	**Example**

Actual Debate

Now, it's time to debate. Use the flow chart below to help you organize the debate.
The introductory expressions have been provided to help you. Put your arguments in logical order and make clear rebuttals to the opposing team's arguments.

Agree Opening Statement
It is our feeling that _____
_____.

Agree Argument 1
For one, _____
_____
_____
_____.

Rebuttal 1
While you contend that _____
_____,
we feel that _____
_____.

Agree Argument 2
To continue, it is our belief that _____
_____
_____.

Rebuttal 2
Just as before, you are mistaken. In truth, ___
_____
_____.

Agree Argument 3
Finally, _____
_____
_____
_____.

Agree Closing Statement
Overall, we feel that _____
_____
_____.

Disagree Opening Statement
Unlike our opponents, we are convinced that _____
_____.

Rebuttal 1
You claim that _____
_____, but we are sure that
_____.

Disagree Argument 1
Our opening argument is _____
_____
_____.

Rebuttal 2
That argument is wrong since _____
_____
_____.

Disagree Argument 2
Second, consider that _____
_____
_____.

Rebuttal 3
It is incorrect to say that _____
_____ due to the fact that
_____.

Disagree Argument 3
The last point we wish to make is _____
_____.

Disagree Closing Statement
In summary, our opinion remains that _____
_____
_____.

Sum Up the Debate

Finish the debate summary.

AGREEING SIDE'S ARGUMENT

Our debate topic today was _____.

The first team opened by arguing that _____.

For one, they claimed that _____.

They supported this by saying that _____
_____.

Second, they argued that _____.

For example, _____
_____.

They concluded by arguing that _____.

Their details were _____
_____.

DISAGREEING SIDE'S ARGUMENT

Contrarily, the other team stated that _____
_____.

They first argued that _____.

Their supporting idea was _____
_____.

The team went on to claim that _____.

The evidence they provided was _____
_____.

Their final point was that _____.

For instance, _____
_____.

Unit 08 Colonizing Other Planets

A. Discuss the following questions as a class.
1. What do you see in the picture above?
2. What planet do you think this picture is from? Why do you think so?
3. Would it be possible for human beings to live on this planet? Explain.

B. Answer the following questions with a partner.
1. Would you be willing to move to another planet? Why or why not?
2. What are some reasons that human beings may need to live on another planet someday?
3. What are some of the challenges of colonizing other planets?

Unit 08   A Learning about the Topic

Should we attempt to colonize other planets?

Read the passage and underline the main ideas.    Track 22

In 1911, Soviet Union space scientist Konstantin Eduardovich Tsiolkovsky said, "Earth is the cradle of humanity, but one cannot remain in a cradle forever." Back then, colonizing another planet was simply a dream. That is no longer the case today. Modern space exploration technology is now advanced enough to make leaving the Earth and settling on other planets a reality. Considering all of the hazards now facing our planet, it may finally be time to make serious efforts to colonize other worlds.

The main driving factor behind **extraterrestrial** colonization is creating a new potential home for humanity in the event of a planetary-scale disaster, such as an asteroid strike or a major nuclear war. Another reason is the fact that the Earth's resources are finite. By most estimates, our supply of fossil fuels will **dwindle** within the next 50 years. Critical water shortages are also likely to occur within this time. Colonizing other planets will **alleviate** this problem. The amount of raw materials—particularly iron, nickel, and titanium—within our own solar system vastly exceeds the amount available on the Earth. A related concern is overpopulation. The Earth's population has grown from 1 billion in 1830 to over 7 billion today. By 2050, the population could exceed 9 billion. Such a large number of inhabitants will put great strain on our planet's natural resources. Colonizing another planet would give us the additional agricultural land and resources that we would need to support this many people.

One of the primary reasons that no one has attempted to colonize another planet yet is that it would require a **propulsion** system that is still greatly beyond our current capabilities. With our current technology, reaching the nearest **habitable** planet with an Earthlike atmosphere and environment could take thousands of years. Likewise, sending materials into space is prohibitively expensive. Launching one kilogram of material into orbit currently costs more than $20,000. Settling another planet would require thousands of tons of supplies, an expense which no government or private corporation could afford. There is also no guarantee that human beings would be able to survive in space for indefinitely long lengths of time. The current record holder for longest space flight is cosmonaut Valeri Polyakov, who spent a total of 438 days in space. Extraterrestrial colonization would require us to spend years or decades in an environment that we are not adapted to live in.

Vocabulary Check

Choose the correct word for each definition.

| extraterrestrial | dwindle | alleviate | propulsion | habitable |

1 to make something less painful or difficult _____

2 to become smaller gradually _____

3 the force that moves something forward _____

4 of or from outside the earth or its atmosphere _____

5 suitable or fit to live in _____

Comprehension Questions

Check the correct answer for each question.

1 What resources is the Earth likely to face shortages of in the next five decades? Choose TWO correct answers.

☐ water ☐ petroleum
☐ titanium ☐ iron

2 What is the primary problem of overpopulation?

☐ Not having enough land for people to live on comfortably
☐ Not being able to produce enough food for people to eat

3 Why would trying to colonize another habitable planet be impractical?

☐ Because we could not bring most of the resources we would need to outer space
☐ Because we do not have the propulsion technology to reach another planet quickly

4 How could living in outer space present challenges for human beings?

☐ Outer space is not a suitable environment for us, and we may not be able to adapt.
☐ People might miss the natural environment of the Earth and never get used to being in space.

Questions for Debate

Think of and share ideas to explore the debatable issues in the article. Be sure to state your opinion clearly and to provide one supporting idea for each opinion.

1 What are some of the main obstacles facing the colonization of other planets?

Some of the main obstacles are _____

_____.

The only ways to solve these problems would be _____

_____.

2 What are some situations where the Earth would no longer be inhabitable?

The Earth would become uninhabitable if _____

_____.

To go into more detail, _____

_____.

3 Why is it important to research the colonization of other planets even if it is not possible now?

It is still important to research colonization since _____

_____.

What I mean by this is _____

_____.

4 Do you think it would be possible for human beings to adapt to living on another planet?

To me, it seems that _____

_____.

The reason that I feel this way is _____

_____.

5 Rather than trying to colonize another planet, what are some ways that we could help guarantee humanity's continued existence on the Earth?

I think it could be better to _____

_____.

For example, _____

_____.

Opinion Examples

Look at the opinion examples about the motion below and answer the questions.

> **Motion: Human beings should attempt to colonize other planets.**

Opinion A Track 23

Colonizing another planet is just a dream for us at this time. Instead, we should focus on solving the problems that we face here on the Earth. For one, we can address issues such as pollution and a lack of resources. The development of cleaner technologies such as hydrogen-powered cars will cut down on pollution and use fewer resources. This will make it unnecessary to leave the Earth from an environmental standpoint. Additionally, it would be a waste of money and effort to try to develop the technology to colonize other planets. Simply put, our propulsion technology is not nearly good enough for us to travel the huge distances of space, and it is unlikely that we will be able to develop such technology any time soon.

Opinion B Track 24

Our time on the Earth is ending, and soon we will be forced to colonize other planets. This is why we need to start making a genuine effort to leave our planet now. Most of all, colonizing other planets will give us access to almost unlimited resources. As we all know, we are running out of many crucial resources—namely oil, water, and land—here on the Earth. All of these resources are abundantly available on other planets. Making our home on another planet also gives us a backup plan. There is a considerable chance that the human race could be wiped out by a major catastrophe, such as a nuclear war or asteroid strike. We will have a much greater chance of survival if we colonize another planet.

1 Underline the main idea of each opinion.

2 Which opinion is for the topic? Which one is against it?
   - FOR: _____
   - AGAINST: _____

3 What supporting ideas does each opinion give?
   - Opinion A: _____
   - Opinion B: _____

4 Create one more supporting idea for each argument.
   - Opinion A: _____
   - Opinion B: _____

Skills for Debate

Read and learn how to create effective rebuttals.

How Can You Create Effective Rebuttals?

When making a rebuttal, you should not only point out the flaws in the other team's arguments, but you should also explain why **your team's position is superior.** Do this by highlighting the problems or logical fallacies in the other team's arguments. Then, explain how your team's position would be **more beneficial** or **more likely to occur**. This has the double effect of weakening the other team's position while strengthening your own. Be sure to use phrases such as "Our argument is clearly more logical because…" and "Our opponent's irrational point of view obviously strengthens our opinion that…" when making your rebuttals.

Practicing Debate Skills

Read the argument from the opposing team below. Based on their argument, create an argument for your team. Then, determine the flaws in the opponent's argument to complete the rebuttal. Finally, explain the advantages of your argument.

Opponent's Argument
Working on ways to colonize another planet will give the human race an additional option for survival in the event of a planetary disaster. Imagine that a huge asteroid strikes the Earth or that a global nuclear war occurs. In both of these cases, the Earth would become uninhabitable. The only way for the human race to survive would be to have the technology ready for colonizing another planet.

- **Your Argument:** _____
  _____.

- **Rebuttal:** While our opponents believe that there are plausible situations where the Earth would no longer be habitable, we believe this point of view is misguided. First, it suggests that the highly unlikely event of _____ will occur in the near future. As for a nuclear war, _____.

- **Advantages of Your Argument:** Rather than attempting to develop technology for the colonization of other planets, we feel that it would be better to _____
  _____.

93

Unit 08 B Debating the Topic

Creating Your Debate

Motion: Human beings should attempt to colonize other planets.

What are your arguments? Get into two groups and plan for the debate. Decide whether your team is FOR (agree) or AGAINST (disagree) the motion. Then, create your ARE: Argument, Reason, and Example. Use the example arguments below and the research from your workbook to help create your arguments.

■ Example Arguments

FOR

Argument

Trying to colonize another planet will give humanity a common goal to work toward.

Reason

In order for any major technological developments to occur, all human beings must work toward a common goal. When that goal is colonizing another planet, people will have a clear idea of what types of technological developments must occur for us to reach our goal.

Example

One of the greatest catalysts for technological development in human history has been war. During times of war, there is a clear goal: to defeat one's opponents. Attempting to colonize another planet will present us with a similarly clear goal.

AGAINST

Argument

It is infeasible for us to move to another planet at this time.

Reason

Traveling to even the closest habitable planet outside the solar system would require technology far beyond our current capabilities. We would have to solve problems regarding jet propulsion technology as well as how to carry sufficient air, food, and water resources for such a long journey.

Example

Scientists estimate that the nearest habitable Earthlike planet is 16 light-years away. With our existing propulsion technology, it would take over 20,000 years to reach this planet.

Arguments FOR/AGAINST the Motion

ARGUMENT 1

Argument

Reason

Example

ARGUMENT 2

Argument

Reason

Example

ARGUMENT 3

Argument

Reason

Example

Actual Debate

Now, it's time to debate. Use the flow chart below to help you organize the debate.
The introductory expressions have been provided to help you. Put your arguments in logical order and make clear rebuttals to the opposing team's arguments.

Agree Opening Statement
Our primary belief is that _____.

Agree Argument 1
We will open by mentioning that _____.

Rebuttal 1
While our opponents claim _____,
to us it is clear that _____.

Agree Argument 2
Our second argument is _____.

Rebuttal 2
The problem with your assertion is _____.

Agree Argument 3
Lastly, _____.

Agree Closing Statement
In conclusion, we still contend that _____.

Disagree Opening Statement
On the contrary, we are positive that _____.

Rebuttal 1
We cannot agree with that viewpoint since _____.

Disagree Argument 1
For starters, we feel that _____.

Rebuttal 2
That is wrong. The truth is _____.

Disagree Argument 2
Furthermore, _____.

Rebuttal 3
Just as before, our opponents are mistaken. _____.

Disagree Argument 3
We will finish by arguing that _____.

Disagree Closing Statement
It is our unfaltering belief that _____.

Sum Up the Debate

Finish the debate summary.

AGREEING SIDE'S ARGUMENT

Our debate topic today was _____.

The first team agreed with the topic and claimed that _____.

For one, they stated _____.

For instance, _____
_____.

The next idea they presented was _____.

To share their detail, _____
_____.

Last, _____.

Their supporting reason was _____
_____.

DISAGREEING SIDE'S ARGUMENT

To oppose the first team, the second team argued that _____
_____.

Their opening point was that _____.

_____
_____ was their supporting evidence.

To continue, they posited that _____.

They elaborated on this by saying that _____
_____.

They finished up by mentioning that _____.

In detail, they explained that _____
_____.

Chapter 5

Creating Closing Speeches

Unit 09 Merit-Based Pay for Teachers

Unit 10 America as the World's Police

Unit 09
Merit-Based Pay for Teachers

A. Discuss the following questions as a class.
1. What do you see in the picture above?
2. What do you think the teacher is probably saying to the students?
3. Do you think the teacher looks like she enjoys helping the students? Why or why not?

B. Answer the following questions with a partner.
1. How do you think public school teachers' salaries are usually determined?
2. Why would paying teachers according to how well their students perform be fair?
3. What problems could occur if teachers earn more money when their students get higher test scores?

Unit 09 A Learning about the Topic

Should teachers receive merit-based pay?

Read the passage and underline the main ideas.  Track 25

To solve the shortcomings of the Washington, D.C. public school system, the former school superintendent Michelle Rhee proposed a radical method for paying teachers: give higher salaries to teachers whose students have the best academic performance. While this sounds reasonable, teachers' unions strongly opposed the measure. Even so, many education **reformers** contend that merit-based pay would encourage teachers to work harder and allow students to receive a better education.

For one, paying teachers according to their students' performance would motivate them to do their best. Despite what teachers unions argue, not all teachers are equal. Some teachers put great effort into their classes while others do not. A merit-based pay system would provide a powerful incentive for teachers to teach every one of their classes diligently. This leads to the next benefit: Students would learn more. Since more teachers would work hard to make their classes **stellar**, students would be more likely to have **passionate**, hardworking instructors. These teachers would cover more material in their classes and ensure that their students are learning properly. Third, a merit-based pay system for teachers would be fair. In most jobs, the most industrious employees are rewarded with pay raises and promotions. Teachers should be treated no differently from other workers in this regard.

On the contrary, a number of teachers' unions feel that merit-based pay goes against the philosophy behind teaching. They insist that teachers are primarily motivated by a passion for learning and that money is **secondary** for them. There are also concerns that merit-based pay systems would lead to academic dishonesty on the part of teachers. Several studies in the United States have discovered that the No Child Left Behind Policy has caused a significant number of teachers to cheat for their students. These teachers change their students' answers on standardized tests because they risk losing their jobs if their students' scores are too low. In a merit-based pay system, a similar situation is likely to occur. Finally, **competent** teachers receive regular pay raises and bonuses in many countries. In Luxembourg, teachers with 15 years of experience make over $100,000 a year, which is a very comfortable salary.

Vocabulary Check

Choose the correct word for each definition.

| reformer | stellar | passionate | secondary | competent |

1 a person who works to improve society _____

2 having or showing strong emotion or beliefs _____

3 very good; excellent _____

4 not as important as something else _____

5 having the skills necessary to do something _____

Comprehension Questions

Check the correct answer for each question.

1 How did teachers' unions respond to Michelle Rhee's proposal?
- ☐ They agreed with it and said that harder working teachers should earn more money.
- ☐ They disagreed with it and said that all teachers should be paid in the same way.

2 Why would students likely learn more at school if teachers were paid based on merit?
- ☐ Because their teachers would put more effort into their classes and teach students more
- ☐ Because their teachers would lose their jobs if their students do not learn enough

3 What is the main philosophy of teaching according to teachers' unions?
- ☐ That hardworking teachers should receive pay raises just like workers in other jobs
- ☐ That teachers choose the profession mainly because they have a passion for knowledge

4 Why does the passage mention Luxembourg?
- ☐ To give an example of a country with merit-based pay for teachers
- ☐ To mention a nation where teachers already earn sufficient salaries

Questions for Debate

Think of and share ideas to explore the debatable issues in the article. Be sure to state your opinion clearly and to provide one supporting idea for each opinion.

1 Do you think that teachers in your country earn enough money? Why or why not?

My opinion is _____

_____.

What I mean by this is _____

_____.

2 Is teaching different from other professions such as lawyer or architect? Explain.

It seems to me that _____

_____.

Let me illustrate this by mentioning that _____

_____.

3 How would teachers change their classes if their students' test scores affected their pay?

Most likely, teachers would _____

_____.

They would do this because _____

_____.

4 Private academy teachers are often paid based on the number of students they teach. Would it be appropriate to pay public school teachers this way?

My feeling about this is _____

_____.

To be more specific, _____

_____.

5 Teachers' unions claim that all teachers are equal and should receive the same pay. Do you agree with this viewpoint?

The way I see it, _____

_____.

A perfect example of this would be _____

_____.

Opinion Examples

Look at the opinion examples about the motion below and answer the questions.

Motion: Teachers should be paid based on merit.

Opinion A Track 26

Theoretically, paying teachers based on merit would be a great idea, but it would be a disaster if put into practice. Such a pay system would make teachers greedy. Rather than concentrating on teaching well, teachers would focus on boosting their students' test scores any way possible to earn more money. Teachers might only teach test prep so that their students get good scores but do not actually learn much. This takes away from the spirit of teaching. A related problem is that teachers would cheat to help their students get better scores. Some teachers would likely tell their students the answers to standardized tests or change their students' answers after they hand in their answer sheets.

Opinion B Track 27

Not all teachers are equal, so of course they should not all receive equal pay. Instead, the best-performing teachers should receive the most money. One reason to pay teachers this way is that it is fair. Currently, teachers' pay is based on the number of years they work. Instead, it is much more reasonable to reward hardworking teachers with higher salaries. Likewise, giving pay raises to harder working teachers would create a powerful incentive for all teachers to do their best. Under the current system, there is no incentive for mediocre teachers to improve their performance. However, if they could earn more money by working harder, then nearly all teachers would strive to teach students well.

1 Underline the main idea of each opinion.

2 Which opinion is for the topic? Which one is against it?
- FOR: _____
- AGAINST: _____

3 What supporting ideas does each opinion give?
- Opinion A: _____
- Opinion B: _____

4 Create one more supporting idea for each argument.
- Opinion A: _____
- Opinion B: _____

Skills for Debate

Read and learn how to create closing speeches.

How Can You Create Closing Speeches?

The final part of a debate is the **closing speech**. This is your opportunity to restate your team's **main opinion** and to **summarize your arguments**. **Paraphrase** each of your team's main arguments and briefly mention one or two of your **strongest examples**. If time permits, then you can even add one **additional example** to strengthen your team's point of view. An effective closing speech can make a strong impression on the judges and give you the extra push you need to win your debate.

Practicing Debate Skills

Use the following debate motion and argument to create a closing speech summary. Paraphrase the ideas and add one extra piece of evidence. Some words have been provided to help you.

> **Motion: Teachers' salaries should be based on the quality of their teaching.**

- **Supporting Arguments:** For one, it would motivate teachers to work harder since they could earn more money for doing a good job. Teachers would also feel a greater responsibility for their work. The reason is that such a pay system would require teachers to be aware of the quality of their instruction. Finally, this type of pay system is fair. In most professions, such as lawyer, banker, and engineer, workers with more skills earn more money. Teachers should receive the same treatment.

- **Closing Summary:** Overall, our team feels that _____.

    First, we explained that _____.

    Our next point was _____.

    Finally, we argued that _____

    _____, just as lawers,

    _____.

    To make our point abundantly clear, just consider the following situation: ____

    _____.

105

Unit 09 B Debating the Topic

Creating Your Debate

Motion: Teachers should be paid based on merit.

What are your arguments? Get into two groups and plan for the debate. Decide whether your team is FOR (agree) or AGAINST (disagree) the motion. Then, create your ARE: Argument, Reason, and Example. Use the example arguments below and the research from your workbook to help create your arguments.

■ **Example Arguments**

FOR

Argument

Paying teachers based on merit would attract more qualified and talented workers to the field.

Reason

One of the main drawbacks to working as a teacher these days is the relatively low pay. This is compounded by the fact that there is no way for better teachers to earn more money. Making a merit-based pay system for teachers would remedy this problem.

Example

The average pay for a high school teacher in the United States is only $45,000. This is much lower than the average salary for all college graduates, which is over $55,000.

AGAINST

Argument

Teachers would focus only on boosting students' test scores, not actually on teaching students.

Reason

Just because students get high test scores does not mean that they are learning a lot; it simply means that they have mastered the tests. When teachers' pay is based on these test scores, they will do anything they can to boost them even if it means cheating.

Example

Because of the No Child Left Behind Policy in the U.S., a number of teachers have been caught cheating by giving their students test answers or even changing their test answer sheets.

Arguments FOR/AGAINST the Motion

ARGUMENT 1	ARGUMENT 2	ARGUMENT 3
Argument	**Argument**	**Argument**
Reason	**Reason**	**Reason**
Example	**Example**	**Example**

Actual Debate

Now, it's time to debate. Use the flow chart below to help you organize the debate.
The introductory expressions have been provided to help you. Put your arguments in logical order and make clear rebuttals to the opposing team's arguments.

Agree Opening Statement
We are firmly convinced that _____ _____.

Disagree Opening Statement
On the contrary, it is our contention that _____ _____.

Agree Argument 1
To start off, _____ _____ _____ _____ _____.

Rebuttal 1
Your assertion is flawed since _____ _____ _____.

Disagree Argument 1
As for our first point, it is _____ _____.

Rebuttal 1
Despite your claim that _____ _____,
we are positive that _____ _____ _____.

Rebuttal 2
What you say does not make sense. Consider that _____ _____ _____.

Agree Argument 2
We must also point out that _____ _____ _____.

Disagree Argument 2
Second, _____ _____ _____.

Rebuttal 2
We feel the opposite. To us, it is clear that _____ _____ _____ _____.

Rebuttal 3
That is not true. We are positive that _____ _____ _____ _____.

Agree Argument 3
Our third point is _____ _____ _____.

Disagree Argument 3
We will conclude our arguments with _____ _____ _____ _____.

Agree Closing Statement
On the whole, our opinion remains that _____ _____ _____.

Disagree Closing Statement
Overall, we still contend that _____ _____ _____.

Sum Up the Debate

Finish the debate summary.

AGREEING SIDE'S ARGUMENT

_____ was the issue we debated today.

The main opinion of the opening team was _____.

They first posited that _____.

Their reasoning included _____
_____.

Second, they presented the idea that _____.

To share their example, _____
_____.

As for their final point, it was that _____.

For example, _____
_____.

DISAGREEING SIDE'S ARGUMENT

The second team felt the opposite and argued that _____
_____.

For starters, _____.

Their supporting example was _____
_____.

The second point they brought up was _____.

In detail, they claimed that _____
_____.

They concluded by mentioning that _____.

Their supporting evidence was _____
_____.

Unit 10: America as the World's Police

A. Discuss the following questions as a class.
1. What do you see in the picture above?
2. What do the handcuffs on the flag represent?
3. How does the United States act as the world's police force?

B. Answer the following questions with a partner.
1. Does the United States military have any bases in your country? If not, what countries do you know with U.S. bases?
2. Why would some people and countries resent the United States for being the world's police?
3. Is it better for the United States to police the world by itself, or should many countries work together as the world police?

Unit 10 A Learning about the Topic

Should the United States be the world's police?

Read the passage and underline the main ideas.

 Track 28

Since the end of World War II, America has used its great military capabilities to act as the world's police by having troops stationed in over 160 countries to **intervene** in various conflicts and human rights abuses throughout the globe. In spite of the efforts by the U.S. to maintain global peace, there is a widespread notion that America exerts too much influence over **sovereign** nations. Is it right for the United States to act as the world's police?

Maintaining stability requires accountability. By having a single powerful country acting as the world's police—the United States—there is no doubt as to which nation is responsible for maintaining safety. The United States is also in a unique position to police the world because it has the most **sophisticated** military force on the planet. The United States spends approximately $650 billion a year on its military, which is roughly one-third of all military spending in the world. Consequently, only the U.S. has the capabilities to solve problems in any country with its military. Lastly, a modern democratic republic such as the United States has a moral obligation to help nations that are in trouble. It is important for America to set an example for the other countries of the world and to show them that human rights must be respected and that **atrocities** will not go unpunished.

The drawbacks of having the United States as military police are many. First, it can lead the U.S. government and its people to believe that the country is superior to all other nations. This may cause the country to act against the wishes of the international community, resulting in strained relationships between the U.S. and its **allies**. Likewise, the U.S. can use its military force to spread its influence excessively throughout the world. Following military interventions, the U.S. government often tries to impose American ways of thinking onto the people. This was the case in Iraq, where the U.S. government forced the country to create a representative government with mixed results. Some also worry that, by spreading its military forces throughout the world, the United States leaves itself vulnerable to attacks on American soil. Therefore, it may be better for the U.S. government to allocate more resources to protecting its own land and people.

Vocabulary Check

Choose the correct word for each definition.

| intervene | sovereign | sophisticated | atrocity | ally |

1. to become involved in a conflict _____
2. a country that supports and helps another country in a war _____
3. a very cruel or terrible action _____
4. having the authority to govern independently _____
5. highly developed and complex _____

Comprehension Questions

Check the correct answer for each question.

1. Why does having only the United States act as the world's police increase accountability?
   - ☐ Because the nation can easily count which countries it has bases in
   - ☐ Because it would be the only country responsible for keeping world peace

2. What moral obligation does the United States have to nations that need help?
   - ☐ It should act as a model for other nations in terms of maintaining human rights.
   - ☐ It should work to spread American ideals such as democracy to other nations.

3. Why does the United States have troubled relationships with other nations?
   - ☐ Because its government and people act rudely toward other countries
   - ☐ Because it sometimes acts without the approval of other nations

4. What occurred following the American intervention in Iraq?
   - ☐ The Iraqi government become a strong ally of the United States.
   - ☐ Iraq had difficulty adopting a representative government.

Questions for Debate

Think of and share ideas to explore the debatable issues in the article. Be sure to state your opinion clearly and to provide one supporting idea for each opinion.

1. What are some conflicts in which the United States has sent its military to fight? Did the U.S. military presence help to stop the fighting quickly?

    Some of the conflicts are _____
    _____.

    The presence of the U.S. military _____
    _____.

2. Should the United States intervene in the affairs of other countries when it is not asked to?

    There is no doubt that _____
    _____.

    The reason I feel this way is _____
    _____.

3. What are some of the dangers of having only one country act as the world's police?

    The biggest problem seems to be _____
    _____.

    To go into more detail, _____
    _____.

4. How do other countries benefit from having the United States act as the world's police?

    Other nations benefit by _____
    _____.

    Consider the fact that _____
    _____.

5. Instead of having only the United States be the world's police, which group of countries should work together to keep the world safe?

    The countries that should keep the world safe are _____
    _____.

    This would be better since _____
    _____.

Opinion Examples

Look at the opinion examples about the motion below and answer the questions.

Motion: The United States should be the world's police.

Opinion A Track 29

As an American, I would much prefer it if the U.S. government worked with its allies to maintain world peace. One reason is that our fighting forces are limited. Yes, we do spend much more on our military than any other nation. However, we do that mainly because we have troops stationed in 160 countries around the world, so much of our resources are being used to protect other countries and not the United States. Instead, we should focus on protecting America from outside dangers. Besides, many nations oppose America's global military presence. Nations such as Russia and China have criticized America for trying to spread its influence and to create colonies of the United States in sovereign nations.

Opinion B Track 30

The global peace that has followed World War II is the direct result of having the United States act as the world's police. This is mainly due to America's accountability. Whenever there is a conflict in need of resolution, everyone knows to turn to the United States for help. Nations would not have to waste time and resources debating whether to send their militaries because the United States has already pledged to keep peace anywhere in the world. This brings me to my next point: Only the U.S. has the military capabilities to be the world's police. The country has one of the largest militaries with the most advanced weaponry, meaning that only the U.S. military has the power to maintain world peace.

1 Underline the main idea of each opinion.

2 Which opinion is for the topic? Which one is against it?
- FOR: _____
- AGAINST: _____

3 What supporting ideas does each opinion give?
- Opinion A: _____
- Opinion B: _____

4 Create one more supporting idea for each argument.
- Opinion A: _____
- Opinion B: _____

Skills for Debate

Read and learn how to create closing speeches.

How Can You Create Closing Speeches?

At the end of the closing speech, you can add the **final shot**. This is when you make an **emotional statement** to convince the listeners that your point of view is the most **desirable**. The final shot can point out **how damaging to society** it would be to follow the other team's argument, or it can do the opposite and mention how your point of view would **make the world a better place**. Phrases you can use include "I'm sure that you now realize how detrimental it would be if everybody (*the other team's argument*)." and "Never forget that (*your team's argument*) will make the world better for us all."

Practicing Debate Skills

Read the following arguments and conclusions. Create final shot speeches based on the opponent's position and your conclusion.

1 **Opponent's Position:** Each country in the world should be responsible for its own national security.

Your Conclusion: On the whole, it is obvious that the world needs one authority to keep the peace, and that authority should be the United States. The reasons are America has the most advanced military in the world, it is a democratic nation which respects human rights, and it already has the support of many of the world's other powerful nations, such as the United Kingdom and France.

Final Shot: If all the countries in the world tried to take care of their own defense, then _____.

This is why _____.

2 **Opponent's Position:** The United States is the only country that can keep the world safe.

Your Conclusion: Overall, we feel that national defense should be left up to each nation. We feel this way since _____.

Final Shot: For the nations of the world to be truly free, they must _____.

Therefore, we encourage all of you to _____.

Unit 10 B Debating the Topic

Creating Your Debate

Motion: The United States should be the world's police.

What are your arguments? Get into two groups and plan for the debate. Decide whether your team is FOR (agree) or AGAINST (disagree) the motion. Then, create your ARE: Argument, Reason, and Example. Use the example arguments below and the research from your workbook to help create your arguments.

■ **Example Arguments**

FOR

Argument

Only the United States can protect the entire world.

Reason

The United States is the richest country in the world, and, by extension, its military is also the richest in the world. This means that America has the world's most advanced military, which allows it to take out military threats quickly and efficiently.

Example

The United States spends over $650 billion a year on its military and has over 470 ships, 8,000 tanks, and nearly 14,000 jets. The nation also has 1.4 million active duty personnel and 800,000 reserve staff.

AGAINST

Argument

The U.S. military presence is excessive and unwanted by many nations.

Reason

A number of countries see the United States military presence as a threat to their sovereignty. This fear is justifiable because it would be easy for the U.S. to attack surrounding nations on the basis of a "police action."

Example

Lawmakers and citizens in nations ranging from Iraq to Japan have protested America's military presence in their countries and claimed that it was a violation of their right to sovereignty.

Arguments FOR/AGAINST the Motion

ARGUMENT 1	ARGUMENT 2	ARGUMENT 3
Argument	**Argument**	**Argument**
Reason	**Reason**	**Reason**
Example	**Example**	**Example**

Actual Debate

Now, it's time to debate. Use the flow chart below to help you organize the debate.
The introductory expressions have been provided to help you. Put your arguments in logical order and make clear rebuttals to the opposing team's arguments.

Agree Opening Statement
The main belief of our team is _____
_____
_____
_____ .

Disagree Opening Statement
On the other hand, we are convinced that __
_____
_____
_____ .

Agree Argument 1
We will open by pointing out that _____
_____
_____
_____ .

Rebuttal 1
Your reasoning is flawed. Think about how __
_____
_____ .

Disagree Argument 1
Our first argument is _____
_____
_____ .

Rebuttal 1
You say that _____
_____
_____ .
But we feel that _____
_____
_____ .

Rebuttal 2
Even though you contend that _____
_____,
it is our feeling that _____
_____
_____ .

Agree Argument 2
The next point we wish to make is _____
_____
_____
_____ .

Disagree Argument 2
Another reason that we oppose this motion
is _____
_____
_____ .

Rebuttal 2
Once again, you have it all wrong since ____
_____
_____
_____ .

Rebuttal 3
We are sorry, but we must point out that __
_____
_____ .

Agree Argument 3
Finally, _____
_____
_____
_____ .

Disagree Argument 3
The third notion we will present is _____
_____
_____ .

Agree Closing Statement
From our perspective, there is no doubt that
_____
_____ .

Disagree Closing Statement
In summary, we feel that _____
_____
_____ .

Sum Up the Debate

Finish the debate summary.

AGREEING SIDE'S ARGUMENT

The motion that we debated today was _____.

It was the opinion of the first team that _____.

Their first argument was _____.

To share their details, _____
_____.

They next stated that _____.

Their example was _____
_____.

They closed up by mentioning that _____.
_____
_____ was their supporting evidence.

DISAGREEING SIDE'S ARGUMENT

On the other hand, it was the second team's opinion _____
_____.

They started off by mentioning that _____.

Their reasoning was _____
_____.

Next, _____.

For instance, _____
_____.

Their final argument was _____.

The support that they offered was _____
_____.

Instilling Knowledge and Skills
for Thoughtful Debate

DEBATE Pro

Book 8

Jonathan S. McClelland

Workbook

DEBATE Pro
Book 8

Workbook

Contents

How to Use This Book _4

Unit 01 Road Space Rationing in Downtown Areas _6

Unit 02 Outlawing Homeschooling _10

Unit 03 Cutting CEO Salaries _14

Unit 04 Free Internet Service for the Poor _18

Unit 05 Extending the School Year _22

Unit 06 Detaining the Mentally Ill _26

Unit 07 Free Trade Agreements _30

Unit 08 Colonizing Other Planets _34

Unit 09 Merit-Based Pay for Teachers _38

Unit 10 America as the World's Police _42

How to Use This Book

Overview

The workbook is intended to supplement the main book both during class and for homework. It provides space for students to take notes during class and to do additional research outside of class.

Introduction for each section

Organizing Ideas

This part requires students to analyze the reading passage from the main book and write down each of the arguments and examples for and against the topic.

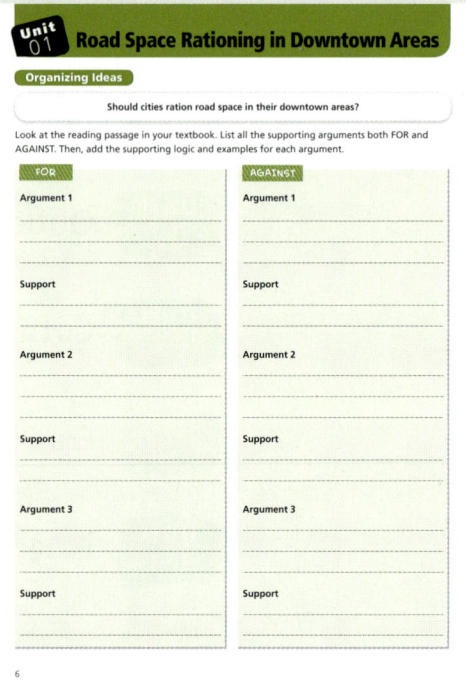

Making Supporting Examples

This section helps students develop their skills in making examples. In each book, five types of examples are explained: statistics, expert opinions, facts, academic studies, and personal opinions.

Additional Research

This section provides students with additional information about the topic based on the type of example explained in the previous section. The information is followed by four brief comprehension questions. Sample phrases are provided to help students create their answers.

Your Research

In this section, students are asked to do additional research outside of class. They are encouraged to find information from magazines, newspapers, or academic websites and to write or tape the material in the space provided. Based on the information they find, students are asked to create four additional examples which they can use during their debate.

Debate Note-Taking

This section provides space which students can use to take notes during the debate.

Peer Evaluation

This part requires students to evaluate their peers' debate performance. Eight criteria are provided along with a ten-point scale for each criterion with a total maximum score of eighty points for each student.

Unit 01 Road Space Rationing in Downtown Areas

Organizing Ideas

Should cities ration road space in their downtown areas?

Look at the reading passage in your textbook. List all the supporting arguments both FOR and AGAINST. Then, add the supporting logic and examples for each argument.

FOR

Argument 1
_____
_____
_____

Support
_____
_____
_____

Argument 2
_____
_____
_____

Support
_____
_____
_____

Argument 3
_____
_____
_____

Support
_____
_____
_____

AGAINST

Argument 1
_____
_____
_____

Support
_____
_____
_____

Argument 2
_____
_____
_____

Support
_____
_____
_____

Argument 3
_____
_____
_____

Support
_____
_____
_____

Making Supporting Examples: Expert Opinions

Expert opinions are usually the ideas and opinions of experts in various fields. Experts are typically people such as professors, doctors, and business managers. Most experts base their opinions on their years of experience doing research and working in their fields. Below is an expert opinion related to the topic of road space rationing in downtown areas.

Additional Research

Before starting your argument, let's do some extra research on the topic. Read the expert opinion about road space rationing in downtown areas.

> **Teresa Ramos, City Planner for Sao Paulo**
> As one of the city planners for Sao Paulo, I worked to create a new master plan to reduce traffic in our downtown and to make it more pedestrian friendly. One of the biggest problems facing the city is the excessive number of cars. Sao Paulo has over 6 million registered cars. These cars create noise and air pollution and present dangers to pedestrians in downtown areas.
> To alleviate this problem, the city planning commission has decided to set maximums on the number of parking spaces in the city. Approximately half of the current parking spaces in downtown areas will be removed. In their places, the city will build parks and other green spaces. These will give the people of Sao Paulo more areas to relax while at the same time reducing the levels of air pollution. Following the removal of these parking spaces, the city will have approximately one parking space for each apartment in residential areas and one space for each officer worker in business districts. Citizens will be able to purchase additional parking spaces for a fee of $10,000 per space.
> By enacting this plan, we hope to encourage people to take public transportation, which will improve the environment in the downtown areas of Sao Paulo.

Work with a partner and answer the following questions. Phrases have been provided to help you.

1 Why does Ms. Ramos mention the number of cars in Sao Paulo?

→ She mentions it to _____.

2 How many parking spaces will be removed from the downtown area?

→ About _____.

3 What will be done to the parking spaces that are removed?

→ The parking spaces that are removed will be _____.

4 What is the goal of the redevelopment plan?

→ The goal of the plan is _____.

Your Research

Find an article about road space rationing in downtown areas from a magazine, newspaper, or academic website. Paste or tape the article in your workbook in the space below.

Paste or Tape Your Research Article Here

Read your article and write four specific examples or pieces of evidence you can use for your debate. Try to include different types of examples, including opinion polls, statistics, academic studies, and general facts.

- _____
- _____
- _____
- _____

Debate Note-Taking

Use this page to take notes about the opposing team's arguments during the debate.

Note-Taking

Peer Evaluation

Read the assessment criteria and objectively evaluate your peers on a scale from 1 to 10.

CRITERIA	Name				
Understands the subject well	/10	/10	/10	/10	/10
Supports opinion with clear logic and examples	/10	/10	/10	/10	/10
Introduces opinions with appropriate connectors (In my view, I agree, For example, etc.)	/10	/10	/10	/10	/10
Uses a variety of vocabulary and expressions	/10	/10	/10	/10	/10
Accurately uses a variety of grammatical structures	/10	/10	/10	/10	/10
Does not monopolize the conversation and lets other people express themselves	/10	/10	/10	/10	/10
Listens attentively and respects other people's opinions	/10	/10	/10	/10	/10
Is able to accept criticism without becoming upset	/10	/10	/10	/10	/10
TOTAL SCORE	/80	/80	/80	/80	/80

Unit 02 Outlawing Homeschooling

Organizing Ideas

Should it be illegal for parents to homeschool their children?

Look at the reading passage in your textbook. List all the supporting arguments both FOR and AGAINST. Then, add the supporting logic and examples for each argument.

FOR	AGAINST
Argument 1	**Argument 1**
Support	**Support**
Argument 2	**Argument 2**
Support	**Support**
Argument 3	**Argument 3**
Support	**Support**

Making Supporting Examples: Academic Studies

Academic studies are research that is done by universities, governments, and large research organizations. During these studies, researchers examine events to understand what causes them and why they are important. Using academic studies is a good way to strengthen your argument. Below is an academic study related to the topic of outlawing homeschooling.

Additional Research

Before starting your argument, let's do some extra research on the topic. Read the academic study about outlawing homeschooling.

Homeschooling Provides a Superior Learning Experience

Homeschooling has exploded in popularity in the past decade, with more than two million children in the United States now being educated at home. While parents who teach their children at home present many compelling arguments in favor of homeschooling, our research aims to determine whether children can actually learn more when they are taken out of public schools and are homeschooled. Here are our two main findings:

1. Children Can Study More Efficiently

Homeschooling allows students to study much more efficiently than they can at school. We have determined that in a typical 7-hour day at a public school, students only spend about 1 hour doing "on-task" learning. In contrast, nearly all of the time that homeschooled students spending studying is directly related to their assignments. This makes it possible for homeschooled students to learn in a single day what public school students learn in a week.

2. Education Is Customized

Perhaps the biggest advantage of homeschooling is that the education is customized. While some states mandate specific curricula that parents must follow, most states allow parents to customize their instruction to meet the needs of their children according to their interests and learning abilities. In our study, we found that homeschooled children scored an average of 15% higher on standardized tests than did children from public schools due to this.

Work with a partner and answer the following questions. Phrases have been provided to help you.

1. What is probably the main opinion of homeschooling by the authors of the study?
   → The main opinion of the authors is probably _____.

2. How much more time do homeschooled students spend doing on task learning compared to school students?
   → Homeschooled students _____.

3. What limitations are in place for homeschooling curriculum?
   → In some states, _____.

4. In what ways do parents customize their children's learning by homeschooling them?
   → Parents are able to _____.

Your Research

Find an article about outlawing homeschooling from a magazine, newspaper, or academic website. Paste or tape the article in your workbook in the space below.

Read your article and write four specific examples or pieces of evidence you can use for your debate. Try to include different types of examples, including opinion polls, statistics, academic studies, and general facts.

- _____
  _____
- _____
  _____
- _____
  _____
- _____
  _____

Debate Note-Taking

Use this page to take notes about the opposing team's arguments during the debate.

Note-Taking

_____
_____
_____
_____
_____
_____
_____
_____
_____
_____
_____

Peer Evaluation

Read the assessment criteria and objectively evaluate your peers on a scale from 1 to 10.

CRITERIA	Name				
Understands the subject well	/10	/10	/10	/10	/10
Supports opinion with clear logic and examples	/10	/10	/10	/10	/10
Introduces opinions with appropriate connectors (In my view, I agree, For example, etc.)	/10	/10	/10	/10	/10
Uses a variety of vocabulary and expressions	/10	/10	/10	/10	/10
Accurately uses a variety of grammatical structures	/10	/10	/10	/10	/10
Does not monopolize the conversation and lets other people express themselves	/10	/10	/10	/10	/10
Listens attentively and respects other people's opinions	/10	/10	/10	/10	/10
Is able to accept criticism without becoming upset	/10	/10	/10	/10	/10
TOTAL SCORE	/80	/80	/80	/80	/80

Unit 03: Cutting CEO Salaries

Organizing Ideas

Should salaries for CEOs of large companies be cut?

Look at the reading passage in your textbook. List all the supporting arguments both FOR and AGAINST. Then, add the supporting logic and examples for each argument.

FOR	AGAINST
Argument 1	**Argument 1**
Support	**Support**
Argument 2	**Argument 2**
Support	**Support**
Argument 3	**Argument 3**
Support	**Support**

Making Supporting Examples: Statistics

Statistics are facts based on numbers. They are usually created by governments, universities, news organizations, and companies. Statistics often show the number of people, companies, and nations that agree with a certain opinion or policy. To show these numbers, statistics can include percentages, populations, and points. Below are some statistics related to the topic of cutting CEO salaries.

Additional Research

Before starting your argument, let's do some extra research on the topic. Read the statistics about cutting CEO salaries.

CEOs with the Five Highest Pay Ratios

Rank	Company (CEO)	Pay Ratio	CEO Pay	Avg. Worker Pay
1	JC Penney Co. (Ronald Johnson)	1,795	$53,300,000	$29,688
2	Abercrombie & Fitch Co. (Michael Jeffries)	1,640	$48,100,000	$29,310
3	Simon Property Group, Inc. (David Simon)	1,594	$137,200,000	$86,033
4	Oracle Corp. (Lawrence Ellison)	1,287	$96,200,000	$74,693
5	Starbucks Corp. (Howard Schultz)	1,135	$28,900,000	$25,463

Work with a partner and answer the following questions. Phrases have been provided to help you.

1. Which CEO had the highest pay ratio compared to his employees?
   → The CEO with the highest pay ratio was _____.

2. What is significant about David Simon's pay and the pay for his employees?
   → David Simon's pay is _____
   while the pay for his employees is _____.

3. Which of these companies pay their employees a livable wage?
   → The companies that pay a livable wage are _____.

4. What is the overall message of this chart?
   → The overall message of this chart is _____.

15

Your Research

Find an article about cutting CEO salaries from a magazine, newspaper, or academic website. Paste or tape the article in your workbook in the space below.

Paste or Tape Your Research Article Here

Read your article and write four specific examples or pieces of evidence you can use for your debate. Try to include different types of examples, including opinion polls, statistics, academic studies, and general facts.

- _____
- _____
- _____
- _____

Debate Note-Taking

Use this page to take notes about the opposing team's arguments during the debate.

Note-Taking

Peer Evaluation

Read the assessment criteria and objectively evaluate your peers on a scale from 1 to 10.

CRITERIA	Name				
Understands the subject well	/10	/10	/10	/10	/10
Supports opinion with clear logic and examples	/10	/10	/10	/10	/10
Introduces opinions with appropriate connectors (In my view, I agree, For example, etc.)	/10	/10	/10	/10	/10
Uses a variety of vocabulary and expressions	/10	/10	/10	/10	/10
Accurately uses a variety of grammatical structures	/10	/10	/10	/10	/10
Does not monopolize the conversation and lets other people express themselves	/10	/10	/10	/10	/10
Listens attentively and respects other people's opinions	/10	/10	/10	/10	/10
Is able to accept criticism without becoming upset	/10	/10	/10	/10	/10
TOTAL SCORE	/80	/80	/80	/80	/80

Unit 04: Free Internet Service for the Poor

Organizing Ideas

Should governments provide low-income citizens with free Internet service?

Look at the reading passage in your textbook. List all the supporting arguments both FOR and AGAINST. Then, add the supporting logic and examples for each argument.

FOR

Argument 1
_____
_____

Support
_____
_____

Argument 2
_____
_____

Support
_____
_____

Argument 3
_____
_____

Support
_____
_____

AGAINST

Argument 1
_____
_____

Support
_____
_____

Argument 2
_____
_____

Support
_____
_____

Argument 3
_____
_____

Support
_____
_____

Making Supporting Examples: Personal Experience

Personal experience is your experience related to the topic. Using personal experience can be a good way to support your argument if you explain how your experience proves your point. However, you should be careful because one person's experience might not be common. This can actually weaken your argument. Below are some personal experiences related to the topic of free Internet service for the poor.

Additional Research

Before starting your argument, let's do some extra research on the topic. Read the personal experiences about free Internet service for the poor.

Gloria Brown, Waitress

For years, I've wanted to have the Internet in my home. Unfortunately, I don't make a lot of money, so getting my own Internet connection has always been beyond my budget. It's true that my local library has computers for people to use, but the library is only open during the daytime when I'm at work. This means that I can only use the library on the weekends. If I had the Internet at home, I could use it every day after work. That way, I could stay in touch with my children, keep up with the news, look for better-paying jobs, and maybe even take some online classes. The only way for me to get the Internet at home, though, would be for the government to provide no-cost Internet service. Until that happens, I'll just have to try to use the Internet at the library.

Edward Gains, Retired Truck Driver

My son got my wife and I Internet service in our home as a Christmas gift. He even paid for one year of service for us. It was generous of him to do that, but I think he might have wasted his money. My wife and I almost never go online. It's just not something we are used to doing. The only thing we use the computer for is sending emails to our children. That makes it easy to stay in contact with them, but most of the time we just end up calling them on the phone. If people really want to have the Internet, they will find a way to pay for it. For everyone else, having Internet in the home—even if they don't pay for it—is just a waste.

Work with a partner and answer the following questions. Phrases have been provided to help you.

1 Why is it difficult for Gloria to use the Internet at her library?

→ It is difficult for her since _____.

2 What would Gloria do if she had the Internet in her home?

→ She says that she would _____.

3 How often do Edward and his wife use the Internet?

→ Edward and his wife _____.

4 Does Edward's case support the idea of providing free Internet for the poor? Why or why not?

→ Edward's case _____.

Your Research

Find an article about free Internet service for the poor from a magazine, newspaper, or academic website. Paste or tape the article in your workbook in the space below.

Read your article and write four specific examples or pieces of evidence you can use for your debate. Try to include different types of examples, including opinion polls, statistics, academic studies, and general facts.

- _____
- _____
- _____
- _____

Debate Note-Taking

Use this page to take notes about the opposing team's arguments during the debate.

Note-Taking

_____
_____
_____
_____
_____
_____
_____
_____
_____
_____
_____

Peer Evaluation

Read the assessment criteria and objectively evaluate your peers on a scale from 1 to 10.

CRITERIA	Name				
Understands the subject well	/10	/10	/10	/10	/10
Supports opinion with clear logic and examples	/10	/10	/10	/10	/10
Introduces opinions with appropriate connectors (In my view, I agree, For example, etc.)	/10	/10	/10	/10	/10
Uses a variety of vocabulary and expressions	/10	/10	/10	/10	/10
Accurately uses a variety of grammatical structures	/10	/10	/10	/10	/10
Does not monopolize the conversation and lets other people express themselves	/10	/10	/10	/10	/10
Listens attentively and respects other people's opinions	/10	/10	/10	/10	/10
Is able to accept criticism without becoming upset	/10	/10	/10	/10	/10
TOTAL SCORE	/80	/80	/80	/80	/80

Unit 05 Extending the School Year

Organizing Ideas

Should school years be extended to help students learn more?

Look at the reading passage in your textbook. List all the supporting arguments both FOR and AGAINST. Then, add the supporting logic and examples for each argument.

FOR	AGAINST
Argument 1	**Argument 1**
Support	**Support**
Argument 2	**Argument 2**
Support	**Support**
Argument 3	**Argument 3**
Support	**Support**

Making Supporting Examples: Facts

A fact is something true. For debates, you can use facts that are common knowledge, but you should also try to use more specific, less commonly known facts. The best places to find specific facts are newspaper and magazine articles. In these sources, you can find all the details of a situation and can read interviews from people related to the story. Below are some facts related to the topic of extending the school year.

Additional Research

Before starting your argument, let's do some extra research on the topic. Read the facts about extending the school year.

> Finland consistently scores at or near the top of international comparisons of standardized test scores. Yet its students' incredible performance is not the result of longer school years or more tests. Rather, the reason that Finnish students perform so well appears to be the result of a greater emphasis on open learning environments, playtime, and shorter school years. More specifically:
> - Students in Finland spend 640 hours in school per year compared with the OECD average of 821 hours per year.
> - Children do not start school until the age of 7, and they are not measured during their first 6 years of education.
> - Finnish students take only one standardized test at age 16.
> - Teachers only spend 4 hours a day teaching and have 2 hours a week for professional development.
> - 93 percent of Finnish students graduate from high school, and 66 percent of students go to college.
> - Elementary school students get 75 minutes of recess a day while American students get only 27 minutes a day.

Work with a partner and answer the following questions. Phrases have been provided to help you.

1 How much shorter is the school year in Finland compared to in other OECD countries?
  → *The school year in Finland is* _____
  _____.

2 How old are students in Finland when they start receiving grades in school?
  → *Finnish children are* _____.

3 How many standardized tests do Finnish children take? Why is this significant?
  → *Children in Finland take* _____.
   This is significant since _____.

4 How much recess time do Finnish children receive? Why do you think this is the case?
  → *The recess time in Finland is* _____.
   They probably get that much time because _____.

Your Research

Find an article about extending the school year from a magazine, newspaper, or academic website. Paste or tape the article in your workbook in the space below.

Paste or Tape Your Research Article Here

Read your article and write four specific examples or pieces of evidence you can use for your debate. Try to include different types of examples, including opinion polls, statistics, academic studies, and general facts.

-
-
-
-

Debate Note-Taking

Use this page to take notes about the opposing team's arguments during the debate.

Note-Taking

_____
_____
_____
_____
_____
_____
_____
_____
_____
_____

Peer Evaluation

Read the assessment criteria and objectively evaluate your peers on a scale from 1 to 10.

CRITERIA	Name				
Understands the subject well	/10	/10	/10	/10	/10
Supports opinion with clear logic and examples	/10	/10	/10	/10	/10
Introduces opinions with appropriate connectors (In my view, I agree, For example, etc.)	/10	/10	/10	/10	/10
Uses a variety of vocabulary and expressions	/10	/10	/10	/10	/10
Accurately uses a variety of grammatical structures	/10	/10	/10	/10	/10
Does not monopolize the conversation and lets other people express themselves	/10	/10	/10	/10	/10
Listens attentively and respects other people's opinions	/10	/10	/10	/10	/10
Is able to accept criticism without becoming upset	/10	/10	/10	/10	/10
TOTAL SCORE	/80	/80	/80	/80	/80

Unit 06 Detaining the Mentally Ill

Organizing Ideas

Should doctors be able to detain the mentally ill indefinitely?

Look at the reading passage in your textbook. List all the supporting arguments both FOR and AGAINST. Then, add the supporting logic and examples for each argument.

FOR	AGAINST
Argument 1	**Argument 1**
Support	**Support**
Argument 2	**Argument 2**
Support	**Support**
Argument 3	**Argument 3**
Support	**Support**

Making Supporting Examples: Expert Opinions

Expert opinions are usually the ideas and opinions of experts in various fields. Experts are typically people such as professors, doctors, and business managers. Most experts base their opinions on their years of experience doing research and working in their fields. Below are some expert opinions related to the topic of detaining the mentally ill.

Additional Research

Before starting your argument, let's do some extra research on the topic. Read the expert opinions about detaining the mentally ill.

Dr. Cynthia Bliss, Psychiatrist

One of the greatest challenges facing doctors today is a lack of time. This is especially true for doctors working with the mentally ill. The current 72-hour detention period is simply too short. To make treatment more effective, doctors must be able to detain patients for as long as they see fit. Longer detention periods will make it possible for doctors to determine what illnesses patients are suffering from with greater accuracy. Many types of mental illnesses can cause similar symptoms. In order for doctors to treat patients correctly, they must have enough time to interview, treat, and monitor patients extensively.

Leonard Oliver, Human Rights Lawyer

Doctors often make the case that they need to be able to detain patients indefinitely. The problem with their reasoning is that they do not consider the rights of the patients themselves. In most societies, the right to mobility is fundamental. If people feel that they do not need treatment, they must be able to reject it and leave their doctor's care. However, doctors are proposing that they have complete authority to decide when and for how long to administer monitoring and treatment. This is an unacceptable violation of human rights.

Work with a partner and answer the following questions. Phrases have been provided to help you.

1. According to Dr. Bliss, what is the main problem with the current detention period?
   → Dr. Bliss feels that _____.

2. Why is it important for doctors to have more time to diagnose patients?
   → She contends that it is necessary because _____
   _____.

3. What is the main problem with allowing doctors to detain patients indefinitely according to Mr. Oliver?
   → The main problem is _____.

4. Who should determine whether a person seeks medical treatment according to Mr. Oliver?
   → He claims that _____.

Your Research

Find an article about detaining the mentally ill from a magazine, newspaper, or academic website. Paste or tape the article in your workbook in the space below.

Read your article and write four specific examples or pieces of evidence you can use for your debate. Try to include different types of examples, including opinion polls, statistics, academic studies, and general facts.

- _____
  _____
- _____
  _____
- _____
  _____
- _____
  _____

Debate Note-Taking

Use this page to take notes about the opposing team's arguments during the debate.

Note-Taking

Peer Evaluation

Read the assessment criteria and objectively evaluate your peers on a scale from 1 to 10.

CRITERIA	Name				
Understands the subject well	/10	/10	/10	/10	/10
Supports opinion with clear logic and examples	/10	/10	/10	/10	/10
Introduces opinions with appropriate connectors (In my view, I agree, For example, etc.)	/10	/10	/10	/10	/10
Uses a variety of vocabulary and expressions	/10	/10	/10	/10	/10
Accurately uses a variety of grammatical structures	/10	/10	/10	/10	/10
Does not monopolize the conversation and lets other people express themselves	/10	/10	/10	/10	/10
Listens attentively and respects other people's opinions	/10	/10	/10	/10	/10
Is able to accept criticism without becoming upset	/10	/10	/10	/10	/10
TOTAL SCORE	/80	/80	/80	/80	/80

Unit 07: Free Trade Agreements

Organizing Ideas

Should countries enact free trade agreements with other nations?

Look at the reading passage in your textbook. List all the supporting arguments both FOR and AGAINST. Then, add the supporting logic and examples for each argument.

FOR

Argument 1

Support

Argument 2

Support

Argument 3

Support

AGAINST

Argument 1

Support

Argument 2

Support

Argument 3

Support

Making Supporting Examples: Statistics

Statistics are facts based on numbers. They are usually created by governments, universities, news organizations, and companies. Statistics often show the number of people, companies, and nations that agree with a certain opinion or policy. To show these numbers, statistics can include percentages, populations, and points. Below are some statistics related to the topic of free trade agreements.

Additional Research

Before starting your argument, let's do some extra research on the topic. Read the statistics about free trade agreements.

Top Export Beneficiary Items (U.S. to Korea) Following the KORUS FTA

COMMODITY	PRE-KORUS TARIFF ELIMINATION SCHEDULE	GROWTH IN FIRST THREE QUARTERS OF 2013	EXPORTS TO KOREA (2013)
Passenger vehicles	8% being eliminated over 5 years	+79.5%	$747,860,991
Packaged medicines for retail	8% eliminated immediately or over 3 years	+98.7%	$687,778,210
Frozen beef (bone-in)	40% being eliminated over 15 years	+24.4%	$264,905,975
Mechanical appliances	8% being eliminated over 3 years	+129.0%	$227,727,726
Almonds	8% eliminated immediately	+104.6%	$170,545,771
Fresh cheese	36% being eliminated over 15 years	+331.1%	$127,287,903

Work with a partner and answer the following questions. Phrases have been provided to help you.

1. Which products are having their tariffs lifted right away?
   → The products that will have their tariffs lifted right away are _____.

2. Which two products have seen the most growth since the implementation of the KORUS FTA?
   → The two products are _____.

3. Which two products will have the greatest reduction in their tariffs?
   → The two products are _____.

4. What is the overall message of this chart?
   → The overall message of this chart is _____.

Your Research

Find an article about free trade agreements from a magazine, newspaper, or academic website. Paste or tape the article in your workbook in the space below.

Read your article and write four specific examples or pieces of evidence you can use for your debate. Try to include different types of examples, including opinion polls, statistics, academic studies, and general facts.

- _____
- _____
- _____
- _____

Debate Note-Taking

Use this page to take notes about the opposing team's arguments during the debate.

Note-Taking

_____
_____
_____
_____
_____
_____
_____
_____
_____
_____
_____

Peer Evaluation

Read the assessment criteria and objectively evaluate your peers on a scale from 1 to 10.

CRITERIA	Name				
Understands the subject well	/10	/10	/10	/10	/10
Supports opinion with clear logic and examples	/10	/10	/10	/10	/10
Introduces opinions with appropriate connectors (In my view, I agree, For example, etc.)	/10	/10	/10	/10	/10
Uses a variety of vocabulary and expressions	/10	/10	/10	/10	/10
Accurately uses a variety of grammatical structures	/10	/10	/10	/10	/10
Does not monopolize the conversation and lets other people express themselves	/10	/10	/10	/10	/10
Listens attentively and respects other people's opinions	/10	/10	/10	/10	/10
Is able to accept criticism without becoming upset	/10	/10	/10	/10	/10
TOTAL SCORE	/80	/80	/80	/80	/80

Unit 08 Colonizing Other Planets

Organizing Ideas

Should we attempt to colonize other planets?

Look at the reading passage in your textbook. List all the supporting arguments both FOR and AGAINST. Then, add the supporting logic and examples for each argument.

FOR	AGAINST
Argument 1	**Argument 1**
Support	**Support**
Argument 2	**Argument 2**
Support	**Support**
Argument 3	**Argument 3**
Support	**Support**

Making Supporting Examples: Academic Studies

Academic studies are research that is done by universities, governments, and large research organizations. During these studies, researchers examine events to understand what causes them and why they are important. Using academic studies is a good way to strengthen your argument. Below is an academic study related to the topic of colonizing other planets.

Additional Research

Before starting your argument, let's do some extra research on the topic. Read the academic study about colonizing other planets.

> World famous astrophysicist Stephen Hawking recently stated that the long-term survival of the human race would require us to create colonies in outer space. But how realistic is his plan? Unless huge technological advancements occur in the near future, the colonization of outer space will remain impossible due to the following:
>
> - No other planets in our solar system can support life. Most of them have atmospheres with little-to-no oxygen. In the case of Venus, the atmosphere is actually poisonous, containing high levels of sulfuric acid. The temperatures on Mercury, Venus, and the moon reach several hundred degrees during the day and fall to hundreds of degrees below zero at night, making it impossible for life to survive on these places without extensive life-support systems.
>
> - The nearest planet that may possibly support life is Gliese 832 c. This planet is believed to have an Earth-like atmosphere and a temperate climate. However, it also has a surface gravity five times greater than the Earth's. The biggest problem, though, is its distance from Earth. Located 16 light years away, it would take nearly 24,000 years to reach Gliese 832 c by using NASA's "Solar Probe Plus" spacecraft, which is expected to travel nearly 15 times faster than our current spacecrafts.

Work with a partner and answer the following questions. Phrases have been provided to help you.

1. What is the main opinion of the author regarding the colonization of other planets?
   → The author clearly thinks that _____.

2. What are the atmospheres like on other planets in our solar system?
   → The atmospheres are _____.

3. In what ways is Gliese 832 c similar to Earth? How is it different?
   → It is similar in the sense that _____.

   It is different in terms of _____.

4. How long would it take to reach Gliese 832 c by using our current spacecraft?
   → The trip would take _____.

Your Research

Find an article about colonizing other planets from a magazine, newspaper, or academic website. Paste or tape the article in your workbook in the space below.

Paste or Tape Your Research Article Here

Read your article and write four specific examples or pieces of evidence you can use for your debate. Try to include different types of examples, including opinion polls, statistics, academic studies, and general facts.

- _____
- _____
- _____
- _____

Debate Note-Taking

Use this page to take notes about the opposing team's arguments during the debate.

Note-Taking

Peer Evaluation

Read the assessment criteria and objectively evaluate your peers on a scale from 1 to 10.

CRITERIA	Name				
Understands the subject well	/10	/10	/10	/10	/10
Supports opinion with clear logic and examples	/10	/10	/10	/10	/10
Introduces opinions with appropriate connectors (In my view, I agree, For example, etc.)	/10	/10	/10	/10	/10
Uses a variety of vocabulary and expressions	/10	/10	/10	/10	/10
Accurately uses a variety of grammatical structures	/10	/10	/10	/10	/10
Does not monopolize the conversation and lets other people express themselves	/10	/10	/10	/10	/10
Listens attentively and respects other people's opinions	/10	/10	/10	/10	/10
Is able to accept criticism without becoming upset	/10	/10	/10	/10	/10
TOTAL SCORE	/80	/80	/80	/80	/80

Unit 09: Merit-Based Pay for Teachers

Organizing Ideas

Should teachers receive merit-based pay?

Look at the reading passage in your textbook. List all the supporting arguments both FOR and AGAINST. Then, add the supporting logic and examples for each argument.

FOR	AGAINST
Argument 1	**Argument 1**
Support	**Support**
Argument 2	**Argument 2**
Support	**Support**
Argument 3	**Argument 3**
Support	**Support**

Making Supporting Examples: Personal Experience

Personal experience is your experience related to the topic. Using personal experience can be a good way to support your argument if you explain how your experience proves your point. However, you should be careful because one person's experience might not be common. This can actually weaken your argument. Below is a personal experience related to the topic of merit-based pay for teachers.

Additional Research

Before starting your argument, let's do some extra research on the topic. Read the personal experience about merit-based pay for teachers.

Shin Hojin, South Korean Private Academy Teacher

I am one of the most highly paid teachers in the world. My salary last year was over $5 million. How could I make such a huge amount of money? It's simple: Thousands of students know that I am an excellent teacher and want to sign up for my classes. I realize that my case is exceptional, but it still illustrates the advantages of merit-based pay for teachers.

Students like my class so much because I put a lot of effort into my lessons. I make sure that my lessons fit together well to create an overall learning course for students. I know the material that I teach—the English portion of the Korean college entrance exam—extremely well as I study the test and its questions every year to help students get a deep understanding of the most recent versions of the test. When students watch my lectures, they know that they are learning material that will definitely help them to improve their test scores. In fact, many of my students score in the top 10 percent on the English portion of the test. When other students hear about how helpful my classes are, they sign up. To me, this is fair: The harder I work, the more my students learn. The more my students learn, the more money I make. If all teachers were paid the way I am, you can be sure that many more of them would work harder to make sure that their students learn as much as possible.

Work with a partner and answer the following questions. Phrases have been provided to help you.

1 How is Mr. Shin able to make such a high salary?

→ *He is able to earn a lot of money since* _____.

2 What is the main reason that students like Mr. Shin's classes?

→ *Students like his classes because* _____.

3 In what ways does Mr. Shin work to make his classes better?

→ *He makes sure that* _____.

4 How does Mr. Shin's situation illustrate the need to pay teachers according to merit?

→ *His case illustrates that* _____.

Your Research

Find an article about merit-based pay for teachers from a magazine, newspaper, or academic website. Paste or tape the article in your workbook in the space below.

Read your article and write four specific examples or pieces of evidence you can use for your debate. Try to include different types of examples, including opinion polls, statistics, academic studies, and general facts.

- _____
- _____
- _____
- _____

Debate Note-Taking

Use this page to take notes about the opposing team's arguments during the debate.

Note-Taking

Peer Evaluation

Read the assessment criteria and objectively evaluate your peers on a scale from 1 to 10.

CRITERIA	Name				
Understands the subject well	/10	/10	/10	/10	/10
Supports opinion with clear logic and examples	/10	/10	/10	/10	/10
Introduces opinions with appropriate connectors (In my view, I agree, For example, etc.)	/10	/10	/10	/10	/10
Uses a variety of vocabulary and expressions	/10	/10	/10	/10	/10
Accurately uses a variety of grammatical structures	/10	/10	/10	/10	/10
Does not monopolize the conversation and lets other people express themselves	/10	/10	/10	/10	/10
Listens attentively and respects other people's opinions	/10	/10	/10	/10	/10
Is able to accept criticism without becoming upset	/10	/10	/10	/10	/10
TOTAL SCORE	/80	/80	/80	/80	/80

Unit 10: America as the World's Police

Organizing Ideas

Should the United States be the world's police?

Look at the reading passage in your textbook. List all the supporting arguments both FOR and AGAINST. Then, add the supporting logic and examples for each argument.

FOR

Argument 1

Support

Argument 2

Support

Argument 3

Support

AGAINST

Argument 1

Support

Argument 2

Support

Argument 3

Support

Making Supporting Examples: Facts

A fact is something true. For debates, you can use facts that are common knowledge, but you should also try to use more specific, less commonly known facts. The best places to find specific facts are newspaper and magazine articles. In these sources, you can find all the details of a situation and can read interviews from people related to the story. Below are some facts related to the topic of America as the world's police.

Additional Research

Before starting your argument, let's do some extra research on the topic. Read the facts about America as the world's police.

> America has acted as the world's police for nearly 60 years. While this has ultimately allowed for greater global stability, it has also come at tremendous cost. Here are the truths about America's military spending:
>
> - America spends more on its military than the next fifteen countries combined, with a budget of over $650 billion.
> - The total known land area occupied by U.S. bases and facilities is 15,654 square miles—bigger than Washington D.C., Massachusetts, and New Jersey combined.
> - In 2007, the amount of money labeled "wasted" or "lost" in Iraq was $11 billion. This would be enough to pay 220,000 teachers' salaries.
> - The Pentagon budget consumes 80% of individual income tax revenue.
> - America's defense spending doubled in the same period that its economy shrunk from 32 to 23 percent of global output.
> - The Pentagon spends more on war than all 50 states combined spend on health, education, welfare, and safety.
> - The U.S. has 5% of the world's population but almost 50% of the world's total military expenditure.

Work with a partner and answer the following questions. Phrases have been provided to help you.

1. How much larger is America's military budget compared to the spending of other countries?
   → *America's budget is* _____.

2. Why does the text mention teachers' salaries?
   → *The passage mentions this because* _____.

3. What services receive less funding from the government than the military?
   → *The services that get less funding are* _____.

4. Does America's military spending ultimately benefit or harm American citizens?
   → *It seems that* _____.

Your Research

Find an article about America as the world's police from a magazine, newspaper, or academic website. Paste or tape the article in your workbook in the space below.

Paste or Tape Your Research Article Here

Read your article and write four specific examples or pieces of evidence you can use for your debate. Try to include different types of examples, including opinion polls, statistics, academic studies, and general facts.

- _____
- _____
- _____
- _____

Debate Note-Taking

Use this page to take notes about the opposing team's arguments during the debate.

Note-Taking

Peer Evaluation

Read the assessment criteria and objectively evaluate your peers on a scale from 1 to 10.

CRITERIA	Name				
Understands the subject well	/10	/10	/10	/10	/10
Supports opinion with clear logic and examples	/10	/10	/10	/10	/10
Introduces opinions with appropriate connectors (In my view, I agree, For example, etc.)	/10	/10	/10	/10	/10
Uses a variety of vocabulary and expressions	/10	/10	/10	/10	/10
Accurately uses a variety of grammatical structures	/10	/10	/10	/10	/10
Does not monopolize the conversation and lets other people express themselves	/10	/10	/10	/10	/10
Listens attentively and respects other people's opinions	/10	/10	/10	/10	/10
Is able to accept criticism without becoming upset	/10	/10	/10	/10	/10
TOTAL SCORE	/80	/80	/80	/80	/80

Memo

Memo

DEBATE Pro
Book 8
Workbook